BUSTED!

THE INSIDE STORY OF THE WORLD OF SPORTS MEMORABILIA, O.J. SIMPSON, AND THE VEGAS ARRESTS

By Thomas J. Riccio

ISBN: 978-1-59777-587-8
Library of Congress Cataloging-In-Publication Data Available

Book Design by: Sonia Fiore

Printed in the United States of America

Phoenix Books, Inc.
9465 Wilshire Boulevard, Suite 315
Beverly Hills, CA 90212

10 9 8 7 6 5 4 3 2 1

Table of Contents

Dedication

It is important for me to take this opportunity and thank everyone who has been a part of my life. I dedicate this book to the following people:

My entire family has supported me through thick and thin and includes my three brothers Rickey, Chooky, and Paul; five sisters Margaret, Carla, Julianne, Tammy, and Renee; my father Carl; and my mother Vincenza—who is really the only person you'll need on your side to win any war.

My business partner Jeff Wolf was skillfully running a major auction house as a teenager when I met him. He's now 25 going on 60.

My lawyer Stanley Leiber always seems to have the right advice and gets it done before anyone else even thinks of it.

All the characters I've been dealing with for years and have made my life more interesting: Stuart Sheinman, Todd Mueller, Carol Murphy, Tony Alonzo, Jimmy Honabach, and even Lowell Katz. I consider these people more than just business associates—they're personal friends whether they like it or not.

I feel like this is a freaking award show acceptance speech! "I'll like to thank my lawyer, Jesus, and who else am I forgetting?"

My daughters Angela and Clairissa are beautiful teenage girls who love me in spite of the fact that I've been in enough messes to embarrass them and my future grandchildren for decades to come. I'm extremely proud of them, and they seem to be proud of me. I love them for that.

Last but not least, I thank my ex-wife, "Babbiez Mama" Irene. When I met Irene, I knew right away that I'd found what I was looking for. We've seen the good times and the bad, but whether we are married or not, we always seem to be together at the end of the day—and that means the world to me.

Acknowledgments

Within hours of O.J. Simpson's infamous Las Vegas incident breaking all over the national news, it became common knowledge that I was right in the middle of the storm. I received dozens of requests for interviews. A couple days later, when the media found out I had a recording of the entire incident, my life went into circus mode. Literally hundreds of requests poured in from everyone in the media. There was worldwide demand from newspapers, magazines, and television shows.

What caught me off guard were the offers for book deals. Suddenly I had four separate offers on the table to write a book about my involvement in the O.J. incident. Three out of the four publishers made it clear that this one incident was to be the only subject of the book, but the other offer really intrigued me. I had met Phoenix Books president Michael Viner a few months earlier; they bought pages from my Anna Nicole diaries to use in their upcoming book *Train Wreck: The Life and Death of Anna Nicole Smith*. Viner seemed very interested in my business, and I had one of my strong premonitions at our very first meeting that we would do something more important in the near future, and I told him so.

When the O.J. incident happened, Michael Viner called me in for a meeting, and the thing that got my attention was that he did not just want to do a book about O.J. He wanted to do a book about me and my life. My first thought was "I've lived a pretty interesting life, but I'm not exactly Elvis Presley. Who's gonna give a crap about my life?" But the more I thought about it, the more I knew it was the only way I would do a book.

The O.J. incident has definitely become a part of my life, but it's not my whole life. This book tells the whole story of me, Tom Riccio, and not just O.J. So anyone who bought this book thinking this is another story all about O.J. Simpson—sorry, you got me instead!

Viner introduced me to Julie McCarron, a very talented writer who helped celebrities like Larry King and Gene Simmons create bestsellers, and said, "Tom, I'd like you to meet Julie McCarron who, if you are lucky enough, will agree to help you write your story." Well, I must have been lucky that day because Julie agreed to sign on, and there's no way in the world this book would exist without her talent.

Sonia Fiore worked on all my pictures, provided all the graphics, and came up with the book cover idea.

Professor Andrew Pulau Evans is an expert editor and made this book an easy read.

Henrietta Tiefenthaler is the editor who battled with me to the very end, without whom I may have never made it there!

Introduction

WHY I DID IT

People close to me who know I've been working on this book have asked me why I would choose to document my sordid past in something as permanent as a book. The fact is the media has already made my troubled past more public than I ever could have imagined. I would have passed on the book deal offers if it meant saving my family the embarrassment of the whole world pulling skeletons out of my crowded closet, but the damage to my reputation and business was already done. The idea of discussing some of the high points of my life as well as the low points just seemed like too good of an opportunity to pass up.

Since my name exploded all over the media last September, friends and family members have sent me hundreds of e-mails attaching articles from various people writing about the infamous Las Vegas O.J. Simpson robbery case. I read most of the stories about the case as they appeared and tried to stay open-minded regarding the public's thoughts on what they think happened and why.

I'm a busy guy, but I've always found time to watch the news and surf the Internet to keep up with most of the popular stories from around the world. I've come to respect many of the popular reporters and hosts of TV news shows. I even read the *National Enquirer* to keep up with celebrity gossip, as part of my business is dealing in celebrity memorabilia. I had some media exposure in the past and was treated fairly well. I always thought that most people writing and reporting on national stories are professional and unbiased—boy, was I wrong!

Several reporters like Anderson Cooper and Nancy Grace treated me respectfully the day the story broke that O.J. came into my hotel room in Las Vegas with his mob, but they turned on me the minute they found out I had a criminal past. The fact that I might even be capable of telling the truth became an impossible concept to most of the media. I was no longer "Memorabilia Dealer Thomas Riccio" who witnessed a crime; I was now "Scumbag Ex-Felon Tom Riccio" who lied to set up everyone involved.

I'm not a touchy person, and my feelings don't get hurt easily. I always try to be fair and do the right thing. I also usually don't give a damn what anyone thinks about me, but I felt very bad for my friends and family members who were worried and had to read all the crap that was said about me in the papers every day following the incident.

I was puzzled more than anything else. Why didn't anyone believe me? I have an actual recording of the whole incident that got splashed all over the media. Why would anyone think that I was making anything up? But as I spent a few nights reading article after article, and as theory after theory emerged about what people really thought happened with O.J. in Las Vegas, I began to see things from THEIR point of view. One story in particular was so convincing that I would have believed every false fact if I hadn't been there to witness what really happened.

Most articles made me out to be some kind of master manipulator, and a compilation of most articles went something like this:

WHAT REALLY HAPPENED IN LAS VEGAS?
Conned or Coincidence?

Let's go back to the very beginning of this O.J. Simpson Las Vegas caper, and in the end we'll add up all winners and losers. A crystal-clear picture of what really happened will develop.

The number one central character in this incident is not O.J. Simpson but convicted felon turned memorabilia auctioneer Thomas Riccio who earlier this year worked with Hollywood sleaze peddler and president of TMZ.com Harvey

Levin to expose Anna Nicole Smith's nasty X-rated diaries resulting in buckets of money for both Riccio and Levin.

Soon afterwards, O.J. Simpson fanatic Alfred Beardsley calls Riccio to congratulate him after seeing him on TV promoting the Anna Nicole Smith smut. Beardsley informs Riccio that he has tons of O.J. Simpson's personal items, and he thinks these items can fetch more money than the Anna Nicole Smith sleaze Riccio just broke records with.

Only problem is that Beardsley has ripped Riccio off in the past by defrauding him with claims that he represented O.J. Simpson. Beardsley had run off with Riccio's money. Soon after, Riccio realized that he'd just been conned.

Later, Riccio makes his own deal to have O.J. appear at his memorabilia show. Then when Beardsley calls Riccio to tell him about the many personal O.J. Simpson items he has. Riccio calls Simpson and makes a deal with him to sign hundreds of copies of the new book entitled If I Did It *in return for helping Simpson get back his personal memorabilia. This book was forecast for certain doom by everyone. Most people thought the book wouldn't sell anywhere.*

Riccio admitted meeting with the Los Angeles Police Department and the FBI weeks BEFORE the September 13th alleged crimes in Las Vegas. So Riccio befriends the police— the same police who O.J. Simpson embarrassed by beating a double murder rap years earlier.

Riccio has stated he is anti-gun. He doesn't think anyone should own or carry guns. So when gunmen came into his room at the Palace Station casino in Vegas, Riccio was very upset at the goons carrying the guns and especially O.J. Simpson for allowing them to show up in the room with guns—which essentially caused this whole mess to turn into the stack of crimes that it has.

Now let's add all this up:

Riccio just happened to have a digital recorder on when O.J. Simpson and his crew came bursting into his hotel room to commit those 12 felonies they were charged with. What a coincidence! But wait, you think that was the only coincidence? Not even close! Let us count them:

1. Riccio likes Harvey Levin and his sleazy Hollywood gossip company TMZ.com. Result: TMZ gets the exclusive opportunity to buy (in excess of six figures) Riccio's recordings of the actual crimes being committed by O.J. and his gang in Las Vegas—an amazingly lucky break for Levin, his TMZ website, and his newly launched TMZ TV. What a coincidence!

2. Riccio hates Alfred Beardsley who conned him out of cash in the past. Result: Beardsley, a so-called victim in this case, is arrested for violating his parole because Riccio lured him to Las Vegas to meet his bogus millionaire buyer of stolen goods. Beardsley is now cooling off in a California state prison. What a coincidence!

3. Riccio stood to make tons of money from the sale of the signed book If I Did It, but only if there was public interest in the book. Result: This whole Las Vegas caper was organized by Riccio on September 13, 2007, the exact day the book was released! It created a mass buying frenzy for the book everyone thought would tank. Thanks to Riccio the book has become a number one bestseller. What a coincidence!

4. Riccio likes and trusts the police. Result: Riccio and the police admitted they met weeks before the Simpson Vegas caper. We don't know for sure what happened during that meeting, but one thing is for sure: The police, who looked like fools when O.J. beat their double murder charges, now have a second chance at putting the Juice on ice. What a coincidence!

5. Riccio does not like guns, the thugs carrying them in his room, or O.J. Simpson for allowing them to come in his room with the weapons. Result: The gunmen and O.J. have been charged with about a dozen felonies, everything from kidnapping to robbery and now face more years in prison than the average person could live out. What a coincidence!

6. Everyone Riccio does not like (Beardsley, gunmen, O.J.) is in a world of trouble, but everyone that Riccio likes (Harvey Levin, TMZ, police, book) has made out great. Who do you think made out best on this whole fiasco? That's right, it was Thomas J. Riccio.

7. Riccio has made loads of money from selling excerpts of his secret recordings to everyone from TMZ to Entertainment Tonight *to even* The Howard Stern Show. *Riccio started this whole mess to make that crappy* If I Did It *book a bestseller, so his signed copies would be worth more. In the process Riccio set up all the people he didn't like, and then somehow he got the Las Vegas Police Department to grant him immunity which means that Riccio cannot be charged with anything relating to this case! What a coincidence!*

Can you see the clarity of the picture that has developed?

Convicted con man Thomas Riccio has once again conned everyone into getting his way, but somehow he is the biggest winner in a cast full of sorry losers. What a coincidence!

Anyone reading that story, including me, would think Tom Riccio is a shady con man who manipulated everyone. But hey, wait a minute—I am Tom Riccio, and I know it's a load of bullshit! Some of the stuff in that article is just a bunch of garbage, but they got one thing right: That whole episode was a series of amazing coincidences.

I honestly believe that this whole situation is a little bit more than a bunch of coincidences—I believe it's about karma, which I'm not immune to. Whenever I do something bad, I'm immediately punished; when I do good things for myself and others, I seem to be immediately rewarded by the universe. The media has more than played up my stints in prison. I have done things that I'm not proud of, and I've paid for them. Then I got my life in order and did many good things within that time. I believe my positive actions have brought me good karma. All these guys that went down over this ought to check their karma gauge, because it seems to be tilting on bad.

The weirdest thing about this whole situation that I can't figure out is this: Why does most of the world think that O.J. was set up (by me or anyone else) when he himself told the *Associated Press* that this whole thing was "a self-organized sting operation"?

Hours after the incident, Simpson admitted to the media that HE was the one who set up Beardsley and

Fromong for trying to sell his stolen personal items. It's amazing to me that most of the media has basically said, "No O.J., we don't want to believe it when you say this was a self-organized sting operation. It's a much better story if you were set up."

Here is the truth from someone who was there: O.J. was not set up. Why can't people believe the truth when Simpson himself admitted on camera hours after the incident that he was the one doing the set-up? Why in the world would two guys on Simpson's crew admit that they brought guns into my room at his request and then plead guilty to felony charges just to set O.J. up?

It would be crazy for anyone to believe that the whole O.J. incident was something I premeditated. I lost so much business over this incident, I don't know if I can ever recoup. In September of 2007, I was in the middle of closing the two biggest deals of my life: one with Steiner Sports Company and the other an auction with the Anna Nicole Smith estate. My company was also in discussions to merge with one of the biggest auction houses in the business. All that's off now because of all the negative publicity we received from this mess. I'm a businessman, and all I can do at this point is try to turn lemons into lemonade. Part of my lemonade is this book.

Individuals and companies I have done business with for years have been 100 percent supportive, but as far as new contacts go, forget it! The news coverage hasn't been helpful, to say the least. To have my past brought up in daily headlines was a shock to my friends and family. Since the last time I was in trouble (and that's been more than 13 years now), I've accomplished a great deal that I'm very proud of. I've built a successful company that has grown to become a trusted name in the collectibles/memorabilia business. I saw myself on the news every night as "ex-con Tom Riccio" and "felon Tom Riccio," and I don't know how anyone could believe that I'd want this to happen to me, my wife, and my daughters.

I can only laugh at all the cockamamie theories that have popped up since the night of the incident. The truth may not be as fascinating as all the conspiracy theories, but I thank God I have recordings of everything that happened to prove exactly what I said is fact. People will always believe what they want to believe no matter what the evidence says (some people still believe that the earth is flat). The media has cynically pushed whatever story is the most entertaining and will get the most attention. Hopefully the facts are easier to believe than the ridiculous conspiracy theories everyone has been fed through the media and other characters in the case.

I can only trust and hope that any reasonable judge or jury on the O.J. Simpson robbery trial will make their decision based upon the facts of the case and not on articles they read or television coverage they've seen. Most of that amounts to nothing more than sheer entertainment.

TOM RICCIO

LAS VEGAS—Sunday, September 16, 2007—*FOX NEWS*

O.J. Simpson was arrested Sunday and held without bail on charges related to the armed robbery of sports memorabilia in a Las Vegas hotel room, Las Vegas police said Sunday.

Police are still sorting out the details of the alleged robbery. That will include unraveling the contorted relationships between the erstwhile athlete and a cadre of collectors that has profited from his infamy since he was found liable in the deaths of [Nicole] Brown Simpson and [Ron] Goldman.

At least one of the men considered Simpson a close friend. One had been his licensing agent. Another had collected Simpson items for years.

But times have changed.

In a Saturday phone interview with AP, *Simpson declared: "None of these guys are friends of mine."*

The memorabilia dealer who notified police of the incident, Alfred Beardsley of Burbank, California, was once a Simpson defender and ally but had recently appeared "sympathetic" with the families of people Simpson was accused of killing, an attorney for the family of Ron Goldman said.

The man who arranged the meeting, according to

Simpson, was another man who makes a living on the fringes of the celebrity.

Thomas Riccio, a well-known memorabilia dealer, made headlines when his auction house, Corona, Calif.-based Universal Rarities, handled the eBay auction of Anna Nicole Smith's handwritten diaries.

Another sports collector, Bruce Fromong, once testified for the defense in the civil trial brought by the families of Goldman and Nicole Brown Simpson. Now Fromong says Simpson robbed him, along with Beardsley, at gunpoint in the room at the Palace Station casino.

Simpson, 60, said he was just trying to retrieve memorabilia, particularly photos of his wife and children. There were no guns, he told the Associated Press. *There was no break-in, he said.*

The Smoking Gun, September 18, 2007

The California man who helped orchestrate O.J. Simpson's memorabilia recovery mission (and then sold an audiotape of the raid to a tabloid web site) is an ex-con whose rap sheet includes at least four separate felony convictions, including arson, prison escape, and stolen property charges, The Smoking Gun has learned.

Thomas Riccio, 44, has emerged as a key player in the Simpson case....

𝕮hapter One

O.J. SIMPSON ROUND ONE
2004

Every single person in my family was very strongly against me having anything to do with O.J. Simpson even though our relationship was purely business. They all made their feelings clear four years ago, the first time I ever spoke with O.J. Everyone knows by now that I had a checkered past, but I had been living a very respectable life for nearly 10 years back in 2004. I had a wife, two daughters, a home, a business partner, and a reputable memorabilia auction house—Universal Rarities. I was proud of the way I turned my life around and built a growing business from the ground up.

One summer day I got a call from Carol Murphy, a friend who I do a lot of business with. She told me that a large scary-looking man named Al Beardsley had come by her table at the weekly Frank & Sons collectable memorabilia show she attended regularly. Beardsley claimed he was friends with O.J. Simpson and was representing O.J. for future autograph signings. O.J. hadn't done a signing in Southern California since his notorious acquittal on double murder charges 10 years ago, but Beardsley said he thought the timing was right. A personal appearance with O.J. would generate a lot of publicity: both good and bad. Beardsley told Carol he thought plenty of customers would love to get their Heisman Trophy footballs and NFL MVP items signed.

The idea intrigued me, so my partner Jeff Woolf and I commissioned a little survey among our customers. We sent an e-mail asking if there was any interest in an O.J. Simpson signing. From our list of 2,000 customers, approximately 200 responded positively and indicated they would attend an autograph signing or were interested in obtaining an O.J. signature. It was just enough of a response for us to decide to go for it. In addition to our 200 regular customers

O.J. Simpson signing an exclusive litho at our show in 2005.

showing up, there would be at least another couple hundred people attracted by the publicity. Beardsley's price for O.J. was certainly reasonable— supposedly O.J. only wanted $5,000. We evaluated the market for items at a live O.J. Simpson autograph signing to be anywhere from $95 for a signed picture to $295 for a signed jersey. There were also extra fees for inscriptions and photos for customers who wanted to take pictures with O.J. himself. When we added everything up, the deal definitely appeared to be an excellent business decision.

The business I'm in is full of self-employed memorabilia dealers who work for themselves, and over the years, I have come to understand why. Most of these people couldn't work with or for anyone else. Several times a week, I hear stories from a memorabilia dealer speaking about another memorabilia dealer, and it's hardly ever anything nice. I'm sure my name pops up in their gossip from time to time, because there were times when I'd get upset at a dealer who didn't complete a deal as promised, and I wasn't very nice about the situation. I learned a long time ago that if you burn your bridges with every dealer who occasionally acts like an asshole, you would have very few people to deal with.

For that reason and that reason alone, I've come to my own set of standards for working with other memorabilia dealers, and here is the only question I ask myself: Can dealing with this guy make me money?

Who cares if he's an unreasonable jerk? I don't have to hang out with him. I only need my business to make a profit. This is the only reason why I continued to deal with Al Beardsley after I first met him.

He's about 6' 6" tall and weighs almost 300 pounds. It seems to me that most huge guys I've met are usually easygoing but not Beardsley. He's a pushy, demanding, menacing asshole. I figured out within five minutes of meeting him what an overbearing ass he was, but it seemed like he was offering a good deal. The first O.J. Simpson public signing in more than 10 years was a bargain at $5,000. So I went for it!

Beardsley wanted a $500 cash deposit, but the day I met him in person to finalize the deal I only had $160 on me and had to give him all my cash plus a check for $340. He was a scary guy. He gave off bad vibes; he made me nervous as he does with most people, but the upfront money seemed worth the risk. I came up with the $500 and got away as soon as I could. Almost immediately, he started hounding us for the whole $5,000. Janet and Frank, the promoters of the Frank & Sons show, were willing to front the rest. They wrote a check for the remaining balance of the agreed upon $5,000 fee and sent it to Yale Galanter, an attorney who Beardsley claimed was working on O.J.'s personal appearances.

Once we started advertising in newspapers and online, Janet and Frank were immediately deluged with hate calls. "I'll never come to one of your shows again!" was the most common remark. There were a ton of negative reactions to the idea of O.J. doing a signing. The sentiment was at least 95 percent against him. It was a strong reaction and not what the promoters of Frank & Sons had hoped for.

The straw that broke the camel's back came the day I received a phone call from a guy named Ben Litvin. Ben was someone I had known vaguely for years from the memorabilia show circuit. "Hey, I saw your ad in the *L.A. Times* that you're going to have O.J. sign."

"That's right," I said.

"Well, you're not going to have him. I have O.J. with me right here." He handed the phone over to someone else, and I heard a distinctive baritone voice.

"Hey Tom," O.J. Simpson said heartily.

It certainly sounded like O.J., not that I'd ever met him before or spoken with him personally. "I've heard a lot about you, all good things. But this guy Al Beardsley, I met him one time in my life because I was told he was a big fan of mine. He wanted to buy my clothes, even my underwear! He's a strange, strange character with a lot of weird delusions. A few people tipped me off after our meeting about what a nutcase he is. Now I'm sure you're an okay guy, and I wouldn't mind doing some business with your company, but I won't have anything to do with Al Beardsley. I want you to know that a check did come to my attorney Yale Galanter's office, but I never approved of this signing."

That was certainly very interesting news to me. We chatted for another couple of minutes or so. "Okay, thanks for the call," I said and hung up.

I immediately called the show's promoter to tell her to cancel the check. The promoters called Yale Galanter's office and verified he was in fact O.J.'s attorney. Furthermore, Galanter made it clear he was in no way associated with Al Beardsley and stated that Al Beardsley was delusional if he at any time thought a deal was done for O.J. to make a personal appearance. Galanter returned the check to Janet, but I had to collect my deposit money back from Beardsley himself.

He wasn't hard to reach. The first of dozens of calls from Al Beardsley started coming in shortly after O.J. and his camps confirmed Beardsley's insanity. Al called me all the time, five to ten times a day at that point, absolutely driving me crazy. I started taping our conversations because if anything were to happen, I wanted Al Beardsley's psycho ways documented.

"Al, this isn't gonna work," I said. "O.J. himself told me he isn't gonna do anything with you, but he would be willing to do a signing with me personally."

Al exploded, "You motherfucker! Don't you dare go around me! I told you I would get it done, and I would have gotten it done. I know people who know O.J. It was going to happen!"

"Look, O.J.'s attorney Yale Galanter told us he doesn't even know you, and he certainly never had a deal with you. I've had enough of all this craziness, Al. I'm not interested in hearing any more of your crap. This deal is not gonna happen with you," I replied.

"If you go ahead with this deal without me, there's going to be some big-time hurting involved," he threatened. "Whether you do this event with or without me, I'm going to be sitting right next to O.J., riding right next to O.J. in the limo...." he ranted and raved. He was clearly a bit unbalanced, and his state of mind worried me.

"I will find out if you ever do a show with O.J.! And I will be there, and bad things will happen!"

Boy, this guy was a raving nut, but I still asked, "Can I get my $500 deposit back, Al?"

"FUCK YOU!" he yelled as he hung up.

Not only was Beardsley not speaking for Simpson, but O.J. had told me his daughter was heading off to college that week. He couldn't have done a show at the scheduled time anyway. O.J. wasn't against the idea of a personal appearance, but the original show was definitely not gonna work out. There were nothing but bad vibes around the whole thing by now anyway, and the show's organizers had had enough. The whole thing was officially called off.

Beardsley burnt me for my time and my $500 deposit, but my family was very happy about the cancellation. Nobody I knew thought that having anything to do with O.J. was a good idea. They were completely disgusted by the thought of it.

I should have just let the whole thing go, but it was interesting to me that O.J. said he was willing to do a show with me and my company. A few months after the official cancellation, I was approached by a guy named Evan. He thought it would be a great idea to have O.J. appear at his event and asked me to resurrect the deal. It was a comic convention/horror show called the Necro Comic Con, held in the Los Angeles suburb of Northridge every year around Halloween.

Evan and I talked and batted the possibilities around for a while until we finally decided to reschedule it for the

O.J. signs a football jersey at the Necro Comic Con that we promoted in 2005.

upcoming fall at the 2005 Necro Comic Con in an effort to make it an extremely huge event. We called O.J. together to make the pitch. "Now listen, Evan," I warned him as I dialed. "Don't call this a horror show. Call it a comic convention because O.J. might be spooked by doing a show that promotes blood and gore after going through double murder charges."

Of course the first words out of Evan's mouth were, "Hi O.J., I'm a big fan. I'm hoping that with your help we're going to put this horror show on the map!"

"Horror show!" O.J. boomed. He didn't sound happy.

I jumped in, "Really, it's more of a big comic convention."

"Okay," he said, and moved right on to the rest of the details. We hammered out a deal that was gonna cost us considerably more than $5,000. We had investors willing to front us some of the money and still thought it was a winning proposition. Al Beardsley continued to call and berate me for a couple of months, but eventually his calls tapered off. I didn't hear from him again.

Months later as the ads went into the newspapers and we started heavily hyping an O.J. Simpson appearance, my biggest concern was this guy Al Beardsley and the possibility that he might show up with a gun or knife and disrupt the show. We had security alerted and kept a sharp eye out for him the entire weekend.

We had laid down strict ground rules for O.J.'s appearance at the show: no media, no talking about the double murder, and absolutely nothing about Broncos or the famous 1995 court case. This was a show for football fans to get their memorabilia signed, period. On the first night of the show at the Friday evening two-hour preview, we only had about a dozen Simpson fans but at least 35 media people.

We had known the media might cause us problems, and, of course, they did. They started harassing the fans by sticking large TV cameras in their faces and asking, "So, how many other murderers' autographs do you collect? Do you collect lots of killers' signatures or just O.J.'s?" Many of our customers, who had perfectly legitimate NFL memorabilia collections, saw the other football fans getting ambushed and embarrassed and started walking away. This was turning into a real disaster.

Many reporters wanted to interview me too, but they mainly had one question: "Why do you have a murderer at your show?" It surprised me that most of the press didn't seem content with reporting the story. They seemed to want to become part of the story by provoking customers and promoters of the show with questions that seemed to be asked more for their shock value than anything else. I had enough and took a minute to respond, "If in fact O.J. is a murderer, why do you have a murderer on your show? You're the ones here covering it and making it news! I want memorabilia sales, you want ratings—that's fine. But stop asking me why I have a murderer at my show and answer that question yourself!"

We finally all came to an agreement: In return for putting an end to bothering the fans, they could walk by the table and each take one quick picture of O.J. signing autographs. No interviews, no talking to him—just a quick picture. I thought this might even work out as free publicity for the event. Everyone present agreed to these terms.

The media left the fans alone for the most part but didn't stick to the rest of the agreement. All the press stopped by the table at once to shoot their video and photos, but they wouldn't leave and started throwing questions at O.J. To my amazement, he answered every single one of them. Suddenly about a dozen media outlets were grouped in front of his table asking all kinds of questions. O.J. was responding, engaging them in conversation, laughing, and joking. He seemed especially fond of one *Associated Press* reporter and actually invited her to pull up a chair and sit down and chat for a while!

O.J.'s agent Ben was fuming and taking it out on me. He kept saying to me, "No media people! I'm going to get in so much trouble with O.J.'s lawyers! Do something!"

"He is a grown man!" I said angrily. "What do you want me to do? Go up and smack his hand? No one's making him talk to them, he's loving every minute of it!"

I have to admit that O.J. did me a personal favor that day by allowing my 16-year-old daughter Angela, who was working at the time as a teen entertainment reporter, to conduct a short on-camera interview for the TV show *Extra*. My daughter asked friendly softball questions about his kids, their plans, and what they were doing now—very easy stuff. The interview was a coup for my daughter, and I told O.J. that I really appreciated it.

On Saturday, the first full day of the show, we moved O.J. to a private back room and allowed the media no access whatsoever. Anyone wanting O.J.'s autograph had to buy a $95 ticket at the door and hand it to me before being allowed entrance to his private signing area. We did well that day with at least 100 fans buying tickets, but the real crowds showed up on Sunday. We put an admission discount coupon in the *Los Angeles Times* for a signing with O.J. and his sidekick Al Cowlings, the infamous Bronco driver who would be appearing for one day only.

Unfortunately, O.J. canceled his Sunday appearance. Al Cowlings was attending a football game in Arizona and called on Saturday to say he was staying there and couldn't make it the next day. O.J. didn't want to go ahead alone after the joint appearance had been so heavily advertised. He knew he would have to answer a million questions about where Al was and didn't want to deal with it. I must say O.J. was professional about it; in return for canceling the last day, he signed a couple hundred items for us at no charge before leaving. Still, more than 200 people showed up on Sunday with coupons in hand, anxious to buy tickets to get O.J.'s autograph. It would have been a very profitable day, but I guess like the Beatles, the O.J./Al Cowlings reunion just wasn't meant to be.

Overall, the experience in terms of working with O.J. had been mostly positive. I had to admit O.J. was friendly, charming, easy to work with, and showed up when he said he would (except for backing out of the last day). At least he tried to make up for his absence, which was more than a lot of celebrities would do. In fact, I liked O.J. Simpson as a person. It was his whiny agent Ben Litvin that I had a problem with. I told O.J. on Saturday night when we parted that I appreciated his business, and maybe we could do other things together in the future, but I could not deal with Ben again. O.J. understood and gave me his personal phone number. From now on, he said, I could deal directly with him in the future.

The press had a field day reporting that our company made hundreds of thousands of dollars in blood money, which was simply not the case. We just about made our money back at the show and later made a small profit from the merchandise he signed before leaving. If O.J. had shown up for the final day, we would have done much better.

It did bring me and my business lots of publicity, but I don't know how helpful that was. When it comes to O.J. Simpson, 99 percent of the publicity is bad.

After the event I got calls from several shows asking me for an interview, and I decided to make an appearance on the *Keith Olbermann Show*. Again the same old question popped out of Olbermann's mouth, "Tom, why in the world would you conduct an O.J. autograph signing and be willing to have a double murderer at your show?"

"Keith, why in the world do you feature O.J. on your show so often? Let me answer that for you. It's because people are interested, that's why. In my case it's customers wanting autographs. What's your excuse?"

"Fair enough," Keith said. The holier-than-thou attitude of the press made me sick; their hypocrisy really turned my stomach.

If I had known how it would all turn out beforehand, I wouldn't have done the show. It was a big hassle for a comparatively small return; not a disaster but not a windfall. At least Evan, the organizer of the horror show, was happy. The Necro Comic Con had gotten a great deal of exposure and press attention. It was a smart move on his part.

The strangest thing was that Al Beardsley, the creep who had started this whole thing, was nowhere to be seen. I was looking over my shoulder the entire weekend, just waiting for him to appear and perhaps turn the whole event into a real-life horror show. He didn't make an appearance, didn't try to get in, and didn't call me on the phone—nothing. He had fallen off the face of the earth, for which I was grateful but also puzzled. What had happened to Al Beardsley? He was the biggest, most-crazed O.J. fanatic in the world. Surely he would've shown up at the show for at least an autograph and a shot at a little harassment.

I later found out the reason why Al couldn't make it to the show. Al Beardsley was behind bars on stalking charges. Unfortunately the day would come when weird Al would be released and the saga would continue, but at that point in my life, I chalked the whole thing up as an interesting experience and carried on with my business. My life had been full of such huge ups and downs that this venture meant very little in the grand scheme of things.

O.J. and I at the Necro Comic Con in 2005 where we did our first signing together.

Chapter Two

NEW JERSEY
1960s

"I was born a poor black child...." I've always loved that line that opened Steve Martin's classic movie *The Jerk*, and I remember thinking if I ever wrote a book about myself that's the line I would use to kick it off, so there it is.

In reality I was born into a large middle-class Roman Catholic family. My mother had five children between 1951 and 1959, and then in 1960 she had a miscarriage. My little Italian grandma on my father's side gave my mom a lecture. She came to visit my mother while she was recovering and said, "You already have five kids. That's enough. They're too much for my son Carlo!"

My mother, not one to back away from an argument, and Grandma went at it. Grandma went home and Mom didn't listen to her advice. In 1961 my sister Julianne was born, and then on November 17, 1962, Mom had twins—my sister Tammy and me.

Grandma stopped by for Thanksgiving. She walked into the house and couldn't believe it. "You have three more kids!"

"Yes," Mom told her proudly, "This is Julianne, and the twins are Tammy and Tommy."

"You have eight kids now! How much is enough?" Grandma wanted to know.

"We're done. Eight kids is enough work for anyone." Mom finally agreed, and she meant it. At least until my little sister Renee was born a few years later.

It made for a crazy chaotic atmosphere, but it was also fun growing up in a house with so many brothers and sisters. I was never lonely and felt a special bond with my twin sister Tammy. She never told on me and always covered

for me when we were kids. As adults we're still close. Not only do we share the same birthday, but her first son was born on September 14, and exactly one year later, my older daughter Angela was born. I've always felt lucky to have a twin like my sister. She's always supportive, continues to have faith in me, and always stands by me. It's also nice to have someone who will always remember my birthday!

Baby photo of my twin sister Tammy and I, from 1962. On the bottom of this photo is our High School Graduation Portraits.

When I turned five years old, my mother told us, "Guess what? It's time for you to go to school! Now listen, I want you two to stay together no matter what. If someone tells you to go one place and your sister another, you stay with her Tommy! I want you two to stick together."

Tammy and I arrived at the local Catholic school and gathered with all the other kids in the gymnasium. When they called my name and told me to get in a line, I dragged Tammy with me. When they called her name and told her she had to go to a different line, I went with her. The nuns started screaming at me, "Did you hear me? You stay there and your sister goes here!"

"My mom said to stick together, and I'm staying with my sister like she said." I refused to budge, and I got taken to the principal's office the very first day of school.

The head nun was even meaner. "You're not a little boy anymore; you need to follow the rules. Now are you going to go where we tell you?"

"No ma'am, I'm staying with my sister!"

The principal was furious and even threatened to beat me. She didn't actually whip me—that came later. She finally called my mother, and Mom relented. Tammy and I were placed in separate classes.

It had been a bad beginning, and things just went downhill from there. The nuns who taught me were scary and mean. I never got to recess because I was always in detention. I had the most ridiculous amount of homework! From the minute I got home at 3:00 p.m., I'd be working on homework until 11:00 p.m. that night: history, times tables, learning to print and write in cursive, and not to mention plenty of religious instruction. My mother was not happy either because she had to help me. She told me night after night, "Your sister doesn't have this much work in college!"

I literally felt like I was in hell; meanwhile, my sister in the other class was learning the alphabet and 1-2-3's. Halfway through the year, and thanks to much hard work by my mom, I was making excellent grades but couldn't have been more miserable. Our Principal Sister Mary Anne called my mother in for a conference. "Tommy is a very bright boy, but he's immature. We think it was a mistake for him to skip kindergarten, and he should go back."

My mother said, "Wait a minute! He's doing well on his schoolwork. I see his grades!"

"His immaturity is the problem. He laughs when we yell at him! He acts like a little kid," Sister Mary Ann replied.

"Sister Mary Ann, I'm sorry if you think Tommy is immature, but he's only FIVE years old. How mature do you want him to be at five?" My mother continued, "I don't agree with you; he can handle the work. He's not going back to kindergarten." My mother and Sister Mary Ann were equally strong-willed, and soon enough they were screaming at each other. Finally my mother grabbed me by the arm and said, "We're leaving."

I was enrolled in public school the next week, and I never knew how good life could be. We played kickball every day, I had a beautiful young teacher (no nuns!), and the work was so easy that I literally didn't learn anything new for years. I was the smartest kid in my class. It took until the sixth grade for me to get as dumb as everybody else again.

*   *   *

With nine kids and a very volatile mother, ours was a not the average suburban home, and even our neighbors were a little strange too. A single lady named Dolly lived next door to us. She was in her early thirties, very pretty, well-dressed, and had a beautiful figure. Men came to visit her at all hours of the night; expensive cars were always coming and going. Soon enough my mother figured out that she was a call girl, but she was a very discreet one. She was the farthest thing imaginable from a hardened whore smoking cigarettes on a street corner somewhere.

Dolly didn't have any of her own children, and she loved all the kids in our neighborhood. She used to have barbeques on the weekend and invite all the children over. For some reason, she was especially fond of my brother eight-year-old Chooky. Everyone thought Dolly was great, but Mom had a sixth sense about this woman and didn't like her.

The 1965 Riccio family portrait with my mom, dad, and brothers and sisters. That's me in the front row center when I was three years old.

One day my mother was more livid than usual and just throwing a fit about our next-door neighbor. "That bitch! She better stay away from my children! None of you are to look at her, talk to her, or go over there, ever again! She's evil!" She wouldn't tell me why she was so mad, but we kids found out that Dolly had invited my parents over to her house and tried to buy my brother.

"I have plenty of money, but I can't have children, and you have nine kids," she told them, "I'll give you $10,000 for Chooky."

My mother leaped to her feet and started screaming and cursing in Dolly's living room, "The nerve of you!"

My father politely said, "We appreciate the offer but we'll pass for now. Thank you." They got out of there fast. From that point on my mother refused to even hear Dolly's name. Dolly eventually moved away, and several years later, my mother saw her in a grocery store with two small babies. No one knows how Dolly finally got her kids. We can only imagine.

Seven or eight years later when I was a teenager, the family was all gathered at the table having dinner, and one of us dared to bring up the day Dolly tried to buy Chooky. My mother had calmed down, but the mention of Dolly's name still got her huffing and puffing. "My children are like my fingers. She wanted me to cut off a finger and give it to her— the nerve! Can you imagine? She thought I'd sell her Chooky, my own son, for $10,000, as if I'd consider such a thing!"

"Calm down," my father broke in. "Right about now I'd sell her Chooky and throw in Tommy for half price."

*　　　*　　　*

As a kid growing up in New Jersey, it seemed like my father knew everything about everything. He fixed everything that broke around the house. He knew a lot about sports, politics, history, and just about any topic that might arise, but he never came off like a "know-it-all." He was a stockbroker/financial advisor and was the kind of man who did all the neighbors' tax returns for free. He was kind, easygoing, and very intelligent.

From the 60s to the early 70s, my dad's financial advice made his boss so rich that he wound up basically saying, "Thank you very much, you've made me a millionaire. I have so much money now that I'm going to retire early." Which he did, effectively putting my father out of a job. He'd done quite well up to that point as this man's stockbroker and financial planner. We owned a nice suburban house with a pool, ate plenty of great food at every meal, and wore nice clothes, but there wasn't much in the way of extras.

Every year until he died, his old boss would send us a ham for Christmas; every year my mother would say, "I should take that ham and shove it up his ass!"

Every year my father would say in all sincerity, "That was nice of him."

My dad went to work for my uncle, who was a pharmacist, and also prepared taxes. Even though he worked three or four jobs, our family was never financially comfortable again. One ritual that didn't change was Christmas. Our house looked like a toy store on Christmas mornings. All my brothers and sisters would go through the Sears Catalog Christmas Wish Book every fall, and we always got everything we asked for. Christmas was truly a day of dreams come true. But the rest of the year, forget it! If we asked Mom for a 99¢ toy, she'd say no every single time.

My mom, Vincenza on her wedding day in 1950. Some people have a hard time believing that this isn't actually me in a wig and a wedding dress!

Chapter Three

NEW JERSEY
1970s

The father of one of my neighbors dug swimming pools for a living. One of his kids took his bulldozer and dug a huge 20-foot hole complete with tunnels in the woods. He camouflaged the underground fort with a wooded roof and leaves on top. This kid was much older, 14 or 15, and the fort he built was unbelievable! He had a mattress down there, candles, and *Playboy* magazines. The kid kept the entrance locked, but all my nine-year-old friends and I could think about were the naked girls in his magazines. One day a bunch of us broke the lock on the trap door leading down to his underground room and went inside to look at his *Playboy*s. The kid was so enraged he took my dog for ransom until we paid him back for the broken lock.

However, we were hooked on *Playboy*, and I knew my oldest brother had one under his mattress. "I know where we can get a NEW one!" I bragged, ran home to my brother's room, took the magazine out from under his mattress, put it in my sock, and pulled my pants leg down over it. Don't ask me how my mother had such a spooky sixth sense, but as I was walking out the door, she said, "Wait a minute, what do you have there?" She pulled up my pants leg and grabbed the magazine. It was the single most mortifying event of my life so far. I wanted to crawl into a hole and die. She threw a huge fit. "What are you doing? Looking at naked girls! Oh my God! This smut is in my house! Where did you get this?"

I was so busted, and for the sake of self-preservation, I had to tell her it was my brother's *Playboy*. He was 19 years old and in college, but that didn't matter to Mom. The magazine, meanwhile, was in pieces in the trash.

*   *   *

For a middle-class family with nine kids, we had a lot: a spotless clean home, nice clothes, and Mom's cooking was fit for a king. Looking back on how I was blessed, that should have been enough, but not for me. I wanted more. It got frustrating hanging out with friends who were given whatever they asked for.

I would tell my mom, "My friend John just got a mini-bike, Chris just got a BB gun, and Bobby just got a whole box of baseball cards. I don't have any of those things, Mom!"

Mom would say, "You don't like it here, there's the door! Go live with John, Chris, or Bobby."

"You think maybe you can buy a pack of Wacky Package stickers?" I whined, like any 10-year-old would.

"No," she said as I ran away from striking distance. However, I still wanted to figure out a way to keep up with my friends and asked my dad if there was something I could do to earn some money. He told me it was my responsibility to do chores around the house, and he certainly wasn't going to pay his kids an allowance for doing what they should. He suggested I find a newspaper route or go to the local car wash where he had seen a kid drying off cars for tips.

I was still too young for a paper route, so I went to the car wash to dry off cars for tip money in the middle of a bitterly cold New Jersey winter. Sometimes I'd stand outside waiting an hour or two for a car to stop. Usually they didn't until I watched another kid hustling and got smart. A friend and I figured out a way to stand out in front and direct traffic out of the carwash. This pretty much forced them to stop, so we could dry off their car and squeegee their windows. Hopefully they would tip us anywhere from a quarter to a dollar. Men were much better customers because they usually stopped and always tipped. Women generally ignored us.

Just an hour or so into the day, my hands were numb from the sub-zero cold, snot was running out my nose and freezing on my face, and my hands and feet were like blocks of ice. I'd be outside drying the cars off, and half the time all the towels would be frozen solid when I hung them up to dry. I always stayed till late afternoon and made up to $20 a day, which was great money for a kid in the early seventies. I spent some of the money on baseball cards, my big passion, and was saving up for a mini-bike until I discovered home movies.

I quickly got hooked on films and spent the money I saved on a movie projector. This was back in the days before DVDs or even videocassettes. I was buying Super 8mm comedy films. They would cost anywhere from $8 to all the way up to $50 for a movie with a soundtrack. My friends would come over on weekends, and we would watch movies in the basement. Later on we started shooting movies of ourselves playing baseball, taking trips, and goofing off, and then watched them together. It was a great hobby.

I worked at the car wash for a couple years and spent most of my money on movies. I was able to put aside some money for cards, and after two years of work, I built up a pretty solid collection. I was happy to earn the money for these hobbies because my parents would never have paid for this kind of stuff. The problem was that working at the car wash all day just to buy only one *Three Stooges* movie was beginning to seem like a lot of work for a small return. One night I had a long, freezing cold day at the carwash and miscalculated my money. When one of my friends and I got to the store, I was a dollar short to buy the movie I wanted. I walked outside again, dejected, and when we were on the street, my buddy pulled out two movies from under his shirt.

"You stole those. Holy shit, you stole those movies!" I couldn't believe it. I was shocked.

"Sure I did, I'm not gonna work at no car wash in the freezing cold all day for this shit. Here ya go, take one," and he handed a movie over.

I was a little uneasy, but I took it, and the next day he did it again. Soon enough I started to see things his way. Why should I work all day every weekend just to earn enough money to buy one movie when this kid could just walk in and take whatever movie he wanted? All my other friends stole packs of baseball cards from our local 7-Eleven while I was buying them. I wasn't afraid of going to hell for stealing or anything like that, but I did have a shit-in-my-pants fear of what my mother and father would do if I was ever caught shoplifting.

Unfortunately my friends, who were a bunch of kleptomaniacs, were a powerful influence. They used to laugh at me or say, "Hey, I'll sell you this movie for half-price so you don't have to work all day." Soon enough I felt like I was the schmuck for working, but I couldn't bring myself to actually shoplift. What I did was switch tags. I got the idea from seeing an adult do it—snorting at a price tag, saying "This is way too expensive!" while replacing the $19.99 tag with one that said $9.99 and going up to the register with it. The man did this right in front of everyone, no problem. I certainly took note.

Since this was in the days before barcodes and scanners, it was easy to put any price tag on a movie and go through the line of some bored 16-year-old girl who was barely trained and then be on my way. I used to switch the tags on movies with sound and color, which cost up to $49, with a 99¢ tag. Later I would bring back the item I bought for 99¢. Since I didn't have a receipt, I would only get in-store credit. So I'd take the $50 in-store money and sell it to a customer in the store for $45 cash. The whole process took about two hours, but $45 in the mid-1970s was good money, and it beat the hell out of drying cars all day in the freezing cold for a fraction of that pay.

My friends all eventually got busted for shoplifting, but most of the time when I got stopped in the store with a switched price tag, I'd just say I found it that way, and they'd let me go. I soon learned that anyone with half a brain who does something illegal probably gets caught once in a hundred times. At least that's the way it seemed for me and my friends, and the risk seemed to be worth it at the time.

I hope no one misunderstands this as some kind of bragging on my part, but I only got caught for various things about 10 times in my life and got away with crap more than a thousand times. If people got caught and punished every time they did something wrong, they'd quit doing illegal things in a hurry, period. I wasn't getting caught. I had all the movies and toys I wanted and sometimes got a bit cocky. I got in trouble every once in a while, took my beating at home, and went on with my petty crime business. I was addicted to having things, and like a drug addict, I couldn't stop.

Even though it may not sound like it, my friends and I were all pretty good suburban kids. None of us were bullies or had knives, guns, spray cans, or any of that kind of stuff. We strived to come up with ways to scam movies and cards, cheat the carnies on the Boardwalk, and get all the stuff we wanted for free.

We were all crazy about go-karts but didn't want to pay to ride them. I'd park my bike in a restricted area behind the ticket booth, and while the owner of the stand was yelling at me to move, my friend would lift a hundred tickets so we could all ride free for a week. We loved to scam anyone and everything. We were just a bunch of punks who liked to have fun.

My friends and I had lots of cool stuff from all our scams including cards, movies, eight track tapes, and we even had our own moped (motorized bike) gang. It didn't escape the other kids' attention. There was a kid in our neighborhood whose sister was pregnant, and the family was putting together her wedding. They needed money, and this kid, who was a few years older than me, knew we had all kinds of scams going. He approached my friend Ron and said, "You're going to help us out. You're going to the store and change the price tags or whatever you do to get money because we need $100."

Ron said, "I'm no good at that. You need Tom; he's the brains behind all this. You let me go, and I'll get him over here to do it." He called me on the phone, "Come on over Tom, my parents are gone, and we can watch a porno movie I found in my dad's closet."

I went to his house and this older guy and two of his friends literally kidnapped me and brought me to a basement. "Listen, your buddy Ron told us how you scam the stores out of money. We need a hundred dollars today. Let's go get it or we'll beat the crap out of you." They twisted my arm to make the point. They were big guys, 16 or 17 to my 13.... I got the point.

I was pissed at Ron for getting me in this mess, but I didn't have a choice. "Okay, I'll do it just this one time. But we need Ron to exchange the items at the store because the workers know me. I've exchanged so many items; we'll get busted if we don't get Ron to do it."

He had totally set me up, and I was happy to return the favor.

"Go there now to get him before his parents get back from work. I know Ron, you'll have to sock him a couple times before he'll agree, but it'll be worth it. I promise."

Fifteen minutes later Ron walked in with a black eye and said, "I guess we're here to raise some money for a wedding Tom, so let's get to work."

I went into the store and switched the price tags. Ron returned the items for store money, and then I sold the store credit for cash and handed it over.

"That worked so well that we're going to have you do this for us from now on," the biggest kid said. The next day I told them that the manager had threatened to call the police if I went back to the store, but Ron's girlfriend works there. It should be easy to keep using him.

Ron knew they were coming to get him and was scared to tears, but I didn't give a shit. He was the one who started the whole mess by feeding me to those wolves. The next day when Ron and I got off the school bus these guys grabbed him and started dragging him away. When they got him alone they told him, "It's over. You're doing this for us now…. Every day! Let's go, we expect money starting right now."

Ron went absolutely crazy and grabbed the guy by his long hair and started kicking and punching. He was so out of control that he somehow managed to beat up two of the bigger guys and the other guy ran away. That was the end of the extortion scheme.

The next day Ron called to apologize for setting me up. I've always been a sucker for apologies, so I accepted and tried to move on. If only I had known what was to come with Ron and all the bullshit he'd one day bring my way, I would have cut ties immediately and forever. But I didn't know, and we stayed friends for many years to come.

*   *   *

I was always a huge Yankee fan, but they never won much when I was a little kid. They finally won the pennant in 1976, so I was very excited for the 1977 baseball season to start that April. My friend Ron wasn't a huge baseball fan, but he was anxious to go to 42nd Street in the city. At the time it was very seedy, a place where you could buy anything and everything cheaply: drugs, porno tapes, hot electronics, and whores. You could get whatever you wanted if you weren't picky about where it came from. Ron's girlfriend was into photography, and he had this idea that he could get her a great camera in Times Square. I told Ron that I'd cut school and go with him to try and score his camera if we could take in a Yankee game first.

The two of us took the train into the city and watched the New York Yankees lose to the lowly Toronto Blue Jays. Now let me explain something: The owner of the Yankees—George Steinbrenner—once said, "A true Yankee fan has a good day when the Yankees win, but a bad day when they lose." I can't explain why, but boy does that hold true for me! I knew it would be a bad day once the Yankees lost.

I had a ball that I treasured with a bunch of autographs on it and wanted to add some more names to it. Outside the stadium as Ron and I were arguing, we heard someone yell, "Mickey Rivers!" He was the Yankee center fielder, a small black guy. He was wearing a long velvet raincoat and was immediately surrounded by fans.

I thought it would be cool to get his autograph, and I waited and waited. And waited some more. Then I could see he was preparing to leave, so I got a little aggressive. I stuck the ball in his face and said, "Come on Mickey, sign my ball!" Maybe I was too pushy because Mickey grabbed the ball out of my hand, threw it as far as he could, punched me in the face, and walked away. My face was stinging like hell, but all I cared about was getting my ball back.

"Lie on the ground! Lie down!" Ron was screaming at me. He wanted me to pretend to be badly hurt so we could sue or something.

"I want my ball back!" I screamed and went chasing after it. Some lady was yelling that it had hit her, but my ball had disappeared.

Ron was laughing at me. "Come on, let's go."

Suddenly an older kid, he was probably about 16, came up and got in my face. He was holding a Boston Red Sox helmet. "Hey man, I got this Red Sox helmet, top of the line. Five dollars," he offered.

"No, I'm a Yankee fan, I don't need a Red Sox helmet."

"Four dollars, four dollars, help a brother out."

"I told you, I'm a Yankee fan, I don't care about the Red Sox."

"Two dollars, come on, one dollar, one dollar, help a brother out!"

Ron joined in, "Come on Tom, help a brother out, give him a dollar, take the hat!"

I don't know why Ron didn't give him a dollar, but I was upset and just wanted to get out of there. I pulled out my wallet to get a dollar, and the kid grabbed the wallet with my moped license, money, and train ticket home in it. We had a tug-of-war, and then one of his friends came out of nowhere and hit me in the face—the exact same spot where Mickey had just hit me! I saw lightning in my head and staggered back while they ran away like rats down a sewer. They just disappeared in a blink of an eye.

"Why didn't you help me?" I yelled at Ron. "They got my money, my ticket home...."

"Hey, they had a knife. They showed it to me!"

A security guard appeared and asked, "What happened here, boys?"

"Those guys took off with my wallet!"

"What were you doing with your wallet out?"

"He was selling me a helmet for a dollar."

The guard shook his head. "Kid, you don't take your wallet out for anybody. This is the Bronx. You need to go home to the suburbs. Describe the kids who took your wallet."

"Well, T-shirt, blue jeans...."

"That's everyone around here. What else?"

"Well, they were black...."

"Anything else can you recall about them?" he asked Ron.

"Yes, they both had very kinky hair, big lips, and wide noses...." said my moron friend.

The huge black security guard was not amused.

"You guys need to get the hell out of here." So we left.

"Listen, you're gonna have to lend me the train fare home," I told him.

"I don't know Tom. Gotta see how much this camera costs first," he said.

I was so pissed the whole way to 42nd Street. "You're going to leave me here, in New York City?" I asked.

"Well, I don't know, depends on what the camera costs me," he said.

"Listen, put aside four dollars," I said.

I had a bad couple of hours and was sulking when we arrived at the worst part of Times Square. Guys were everywhere saying, "Uppers, downers, reds, pinks, yellows, hot hos, what you need?" Ron looked for the right person to approach.

A small Hispanic guy came up to us and said, "Whatever your vice, I got it nice. What you boys want?"

"You got a Minolta camera, XL 76-B?" Ron challenged.

"I got a Minolta 76 A, B and C!" the guy answered. "How much money you got?"

"Well, I know they sell for $500, but I only have $57."

"Lucky you, we're having a sale today. Exactly $57 for a Minolta XL 76-B! Just for you!"

He led us to the front of a porno shop and leaned in the door. "Hey, you got a Minolta XL 76-B in there?" he shouted and waited. "Sure enough, we got just one left," he told my friend. "Now give me your money, and I'll go get it. Hey," he added when Ron hesitated. "Come on, it's brand new in the box. I gotta run all the way upstairs and pay the man to get it. So you gotta pay me first!"

Ron handed over the money, and the guy told him, "I'll be back in two minutes. You wait right here. Five minutes, tops."

He disappeared into the shop. "Ron, I hope you left aside four bucks for the trip home," I said.

"My girlfriend is going to be so happy! I finally got it for her! Maybe she'll let me in her pants!" He was trying to high-five me; I wasn't so sure. Ten minutes passed, then fifteen.

"Hey Ron, this guy isn't coming back," I pointed out.

"Oh shit, I'm going in there and get my money back!" Ron said, and marched into the shop. The owner stopped us both at the door.

"What the hell do you think you're doing? You're not 21 years old! You're not coming in here!"

"That guy took my money! I bought a Minolta camera from him, and he came in here to get it."

"Does this look like a fucking camera shop to you? I don't give a shit what happened. You kids ain't coming in here!"

"Well, can you just have that little Puerto Rican guy come back out here?" Ron asked.

"What? That guy ran out the back door 15 minutes ago. He's halfway to Harlem by now. Get the hell out of here!"

We didn't have a dime, and I didn't have a ticket home. Our very first trip to New York on our own hadn't turned out so well. "I'll be homeless on the street before I call my mother," I told Ron. "If she knew I cut school...."

We wound up taking turns darting into restaurants and stealing tip money off the tables until we had the four dollars to get me home. In the last place, the busboy saw Ron steal a tip and started chasing us. We ran like hell out of there, got on the train, and started for home.

"Don't tell my mother, whatever you do, don't tell my mother any of this. If she knew I'd lost $57.... No one needs to know about this," Ron kept repeating.

"Don't worry, I don't want my mother to know either," I told him.

It was dark when we got home. We were late and missed dinner, a big problem in an Italian family. We could do whatever we wanted after school, but we were not allowed to miss dinner. By the time we walked into his house at 8:00 p.m., his mother jumped up and yelled, "Where the hell have you been?"

I'll be damned if the first words out of Ron's mouth weren't "we went to a Yankee game, and Tom got hit by Mickey Rivers," after begging me the whole way home to keep my mouth shut, which I would have.

"Oh yeah? Well, I'm Mickey Mantle!" his mother screamed as she whacked him in the head. Then she slammed the door on me. I went home and got whacked for missing dinner, but that was no big deal after all the day's bullshit.

*   *   *

As a kid in high school, I don't know exactly how you would categorize me. I wasn't a nerd, but I certainly wasn't a jock or in the popular crowd. The most common comment people would say to me was, "How come your twin sister Tammy is so popular and beautiful, and you're you?" People thought that because we were twins we had to be alike. Lucky for Tammy that wasn't the case.

The friends I hung out with weren't bullies or trouble-makers. We were all just on a constant prowl for good times, but sometimes trouble would find us.

After high school, all my childhood friends (even Ron) turned out to be decent adults. What we were doing didn't seem bad at the time, because we were just kids being kids. As for my eight brothers and sisters, every single one of them graduated from college. All of them became very successful professionals. Most of them are millionaires today, and none of them ever had any brushes with the law. Except for me—I'm not a millionaire and I wasn't quite done with the delinquent behavior.

Chapter Four

ATLANTIC CITY/LAS VEGAS/LOS ANGELES 1978 - 1981

Collecting baseball cards was something every kid did for a while, but most of the guys I knew eventually outgrew it. They found other interests and got rid of their collections, but I never outgrew my hobby. A few of my friends were embarrassed that I still collected cards, but I didn't care what anyone thought. Baseball card conventions were held in New York City a couple times a year, and the idea that cards could be a way to make money intrigued me even though it was not a well-known business in the late 70s.

I placed a "buying baseball cards" ad in my local newspaper, and a lady with a refrigerator box full of cards came to my house. Her collection must have been worth at least $1,000, but I learned early on how to act when buying a collection. You never make the first offer. Wait and see where they're at to start. "So, what do you want for your cards?" I asked.

"Well, it cost me five dollars in gas to get here; I'd really like to get at least twenty. My brother probably spent more than that on these as a kid before he died in the war."

"You got it," I said and gave her $20.

I took the collection to sell at the annual card show in New York. In those days it was still more like a hobby and not the multi-billion-dollar industry cards would become by the mid-80s. I took the bus to Manhattan and paid my dollar to get into the show. I got a ticket in return. I asked what the ticket was for, and the lady at the door said, "Now you can get an autograph."

"Oh yeah? From who?" I asked. I went around the corner, and there was Mickey Mantle sitting at a table surrounded by fans, just talking away.

"I remember back in 1960 when you hit that 500-foot home run!" one man was saying to him.

"Oh yeah, I had a few drinks that day," Mickey laughed, "but I really felt strong later on." He was just sitting there, shooting the breeze with whoever came by, and signing their cards. This experience was free with the payment of a dollar admission. I got an 8 x10 photo then waited in the short line, and Mickey Mantle was as friendly as could be when I approached. "What's your name, son?" he asked.

"Tommy," I told him. TO TOMMY, BEST WISHES, MICKEY MANTLE, he wrote.

I saw The Mick 10 years later at another show where it cost $195 for his autograph. One of his fans tried to tell him a story, "Hey Mick, I remember when...." and a security guy elbowed him out of the way.

"Mick don't talk to nobody," he said coldly.

Another fan asked, "Hi Mickey, can you make that to John?"

"Mick don't personalize nothing," the security guy told another fan.

I talked to a promoter I knew in the business about Mickey Mantle's appearance shortly afterward and learned that he had been paid $50,000 for his appearance, plus a percentage of the autograph proceeds. No talking, no personalizing. I thought back to 1979 when you could sit around and reminisce with Mickey Mantle all you wanted for a dollar. That's what 10 years did to the autograph/ collectible/ card business.

With the money I made selling the collection at that show, I bought an old Oldsmobile complete with a first-generation cassette tape player. I went to the store and switched out price tags on everything, so I wound up with expensive Jensen speakers for only $9.99. The stereo system was certainly worth more than the car itself.

I headed down to Atlantic City with a friend of mine for a quick trip just before graduation. You had to be 18 years old to gamble and I was only 17, but that didn't stop me. I had been there plenty of times and usually lost. On this trip I brought about $100 with me. My friend and I lost every cent we had. We didn't have enough money to put gas in the car to drive home, but I wasn't about to call my parents for help.

We walked around the casino until we saw a guy sitting in front of a machine, surrounded by a dozen cups full of Susan B. Anthony dollar coins. He must have just hit the jackpot. My friend walked behind the machine, grabbed one of the cups resting on top, and asked, "Will this get us home?" There was more than $200 in that cup. We split the money, and I wound up winning $4,800 playing blackjack with my share of the money he lifted.

I graduated and moved out of my parents' house the very next day. I found a little one-bedroom apartment about five miles from their home for $200 a month. I thought I was all set with my winnings from Atlantic City. Three or four of my friends were supposed to be living there too, but every one of them said, "My mom said we're going to have other bills…phone, electricity. I'm living good at home. I'm staying where I am."

After living alone in my new place for a week and eating McDonald's every day, I realized how right they were. I missed my mom's good cooking, but I was free to be with girls every day, and that was worth a lot to me. Instead of moving in and paying rent, my friends came over and hung out and threw parties at my place every night. My neighbors, an elderly couple across the hall, were pissed off about this. They didn't like all those punks partying, yelling, and making noise. They were constantly calling the cops on us for noise violations, but we didn't care. I was finally out of my parents' house, like a bird out of a cage, and the party was on.

I came home one night tired and thinking of sleep, only to find a raging party going on in my own apartment. My friends were fooling around with my movie projector and playing a porno movie directly onto the old neighbors' huge picture window. From outside it looked like a pornographic drive-in movie. I raced into the apartment building just ahead of the cops. Apparently the old lady had walked into her living room, seen a huge penis projected on her living room wall, and almost had a heart attack. The only thing the cops wanted to know was whose name was on the lease; it was mine, of course. I got evicted very quickly.

I didn't know what to do. I needed money, so I headed to Atlantic City to play blackjack. I had developed a scam system that couldn't lose. As a kid on the boardwalk, my friends and I cheated every carny in town. The most popular game on the boardwalk was called the Wheel of Fortune. You placed a 25-cent bet on a number, and you win your choice of any prize in the stand if the wheel stops on your number. My friends would distract the guy working the stand as the wheel stopped, and then I would place my quarter on the winning number after the marker landed on a number. It's easy to place a winning bet if you can place your bet after you know the winning number. If only I could do that in Atlantic City. Then I thought, why not?

Here's how I did it. I bought ten red five-dollar chips and one dark pink five-hundred-dollar chip. It was hard to tell them apart in the dim light. I always sat in the number one seat to play and bet two five-dollar chips per hand until I hit blackjack or 21. When the dealer turned his head to the number seven seat on the other side of the table, my friend would delay his call a few seconds to give me plenty of time to take away the stack of two red chips with one hand and replace it with one red chip and a pink one underneath. I could make the switch in one quick, smooth motion. I'd then act very happy, and the dealer would see that I had bet $505 after I won. I practiced the timing and got pretty good at sleight of hand; no one ever noticed. I became so skilled and my timing was so good I was able to do it all on my own, leaving me a larger share. I pulled this stunt two or three times a day, several times a week.

In the dozens of times I switched out chips, no one ever caught on, except one day a woman sitting on the stool next to me pinched me on my thigh right after I'd made the switch and said, "You're giving me half of that, isn't that right?"

Half was better than none, so I swallowed and said, "Yeah, sure." When we left the table I had to give her half the money.

Unfortunately for me there were only four or five casinos in Atlantic City at that time. Security wasn't nearly what it is in casinos now. This was around 1980 and supposedly they had "eyes in the sky," but they never approached me about catching the switch of chips on tape. Today they would probably have me taped from five different angles. The one thing I feared were the pit bosses, because they were starting to give me looks whenever I showed up. I had to make sure they weren't watching my table when I made the switch. They could never catch me red-handed, but one day a floor manager came over to me and said, "We don't know what the hell you're doing, but we don't want you in here anymore." That jig was pretty much up, and I was still only 17. I wasn't even supposed to be gambling at all! However, it was the most surefire way I knew to make money.

Even though I knew dammed well what I was doing was wrong, it never bothered me to scam casinos for some of their profits. I would never hurt anyone, break into a house or car, or anything like that, but I definitely wanted money the easy way. Cheating casinos, in my mind, wasn't hurting anybody. I justified my screwed-up actions by vilifying the victims or telling myself it was a victimless crime so that I could live with myself and the decisions I made.

I was running out of options in Atlantic City. It occurred to me that I should head out to Las Vegas for a while. I flew to Sin City and got a hotel room. I was young and cocky and out on my own; it all seemed like a great new world.

Vegas was heaven to me because I had never seen so many casinos. By the end of my very first day, I was up nine grand by switching out thousand-dollar chips every time I hit 21. On my second day, I once again did my switch, collected my winnings and left. However, security was a little savvier in Las Vegas. The casino sent some staffers to follow me to the next place I stopped. They watched me switch out the chips when I hit 21 and caught me red-handed. I was arrested on bunco or fraud, some charge like that. The cops confiscated every cent I had, all $9,000 or so.

My parents had no idea where I was. Only a few friends knew I was in Vegas while I sat in a jail cell waiting for my preliminary hearing. I didn't have any money and couldn't make bail. A friend of mine back in Jersey called my parents' house when I didn't return the day I was supposed to, and everyone got worried. Eventually they figured out where I was, and my family rallied together behind me and wired some money; I was released on bail.

My uncle had a friend in Vegas, a nice old guy, and I went to help him fix up his house while I waited for my hearing. I wasn't overly worried; I hung out at the Circus Circus casino at night and met some girls my age. They were kind of hard girls who drank a lot, did drugs, and wanted to gamble. Vegas was different in those days—hookers would literally assault any man walking alone on the Strip. I wasn't into all that. I liked regular girls, but once again the ones I met had lots of issues. I also had my own problems at the time.

I was given probation for the scam with the chips in the casino. The amazing thing was that the police gave me back most of my money after the hearing, about $7,000. I knew it was time to grow up and do other things with my life. The scams had to stop; I needed to go to school or get a real job and set some life goals. I was interested in television production and looked into a school called the Don Martin School of Communications in Los Angeles. So, I bought a car and drove to Hollywood.

A man I met through the school knew I was looking for an apartment and was willing to share his place with me. It was a tiny place; my allotted space was literally the size of a closet, but he was charging me only $150 per month.

The school gave me a career aptitude test the first week I was there, and the results showed I would make a good detective or police officer. I don't know how they arrived at this conclusion, but there you have it. A teacher passed on the results to a security company called Burns Security, and they hired me. I was posted at Universal Studios, which was a very cool job assignment for a kid from Jersey.

My job was to walk around and do fire and security checks at about 20 different sound stages and prop warehouses. During the day they shot all kinds of television shows and movies; I saw Barbara Eden from *I Dream of Jeannie* who I'd had the biggest crush on when I was young. I also saw John Belushi and lots of other famous faces. It was great!

The job itself was easy. The strictest rule Burns had was that their guards were not allowed to use the bathroom without checking in with the Sergeant's office first. I sat at a desk outside an editing office at night except when I made my rounds and usually passed the time reading my baseball magazines. All in all it was a great job. I was making decent money for a kid my age and couldn't have worked at a better location. I had been doing very well, and after a few months without a single write-up incident, I was up for a promotion to "on location security." Traveling on location would mean a huge raise.

Life was great until the one night I left my post for literally a minute to run across the hall and take a piss. Some girl on kart patrol reported me, and the lieutenant called me to ask, "Tom, did you just go to the bathroom?"

I didn't want to lie to him and admitted, "Yes, I left the door open. I was gone for less than a minute." The next day I received a write-up, which meant I had to work for another six months without an incident before I could think about promotion.

I was so mad that I refused to sign the write-up slip. I started backpedaling like crazy. "I didn't go to the bathroom. I just stood up and walked around!" They weren't buying it, and by the end of the meeting, they sent me back to Burns home office where they told me I had been reassigned to a Ralph's supermarket located in a seedy section of Inglewood. It was quite a comedown from Universal Studios.

I went to the store and wasn't there five minutes when the neighborhood gang-bangers oriented me on the way they expected me to act while I was in their 'hood. They made it very clear that if I valued my health, I'd turn my head the other way when one of their "homies" walked out of the store without paying. I lasted less than an hour at my new post. I left Burns and never even bothered to return my uniform.

It was now October of 1981. I wasn't sure what to do next, but the Yankees were playing the Dodgers in Los Angeles that year in the World Series. It was a huge Series— Fernandomania was in full swing. I wasn't about to leave California without going to see my team in the World Series. A friend and I stayed up all night at Dodger Stadium to camp out for tickets, and at about ten o'clock in the morning, they announced to the huge crowd there were no more tickets. As We were walking away very discouraged, a guy approached me and said, "Want some tickets? A hundred dollars apiece?"

"What's the deal, how'd you get those?" I asked.

He explained that they were special tickets set aside for handicapped fans. You were only allowed to buy them if you were with someone in a wheelchair. So, with that in mind, my friend and I went straight to the hospital, "borrowed" a wheelchair and returned to Dodger Stadium where they werre happy to sel us the special tickets. We went into the first game and snuck down to the clubhouse entrance where there was a herd of reporters waiting to get in to interview the players. No one could get inside the clubhouse because the team was in the middle of a meeting. Then a security guy barked at us, "The doors will be opening soon. Nobody allowed in the clubhouse without their passes on!"

Members of the press were pushing and shoving behind us, and we were being crushed. A man jammed up in front of me had two passes sticking out of his back pocket, and when I got shoved against him I grabbed them. I never even saw his face; I only saw two laminated passes. I gave one to my friend, and the two of us entered the clubhouse and had the greatest time any fan could dream of. I gave my friend my movie camera, and he filmed me interviewing all my favorite Yankee players. I even got to speak with some old-time legends like Yogi Berra and Sandy Koufax!

On our way out we saw some poor guy screaming, "I really am with the *Washington Post*. I'm going to get fired! You have to let me in!" I looked down and my pass said *The Washington Post*. I figured we had his passes and felt sorry for that guy, but there wasn't much I could do at that point.

The pass was good for the whole World Series—every game. I wouldn't have missed that experience for anything, but I had no job and was running out of money. My friends were constantly calling to tell me they missed me. I missed them too. My West Coast experience was over. I headed home.

Chapter Five

NEW YORK/FLORIDA/ FEDERAL PRISON 1982 - 1984

I returned to New Jersey and took stock of my life. The only possession of any value I owned was my baseball card collection. It killed me to do it, but I knew I was going to have to sell off part of it. I needed to get my own place again—fast!

Baseball card shows still weren't popular at that time, but a friend of mine and I went to a coin show at a big hotel in New York where people sometimes dealt in cards. As soon as we arrived, I met a man who bought some of my cards for very little money, maybe 10 percent of their book value. I needed the cash and sadly watched as a chunk of my collection was placed in a large attaché case along with all his rare coins.

As I waited in the lobby for my friend to come out of the men's room, I was suffering from a bad case of seller's remorse. Then I saw the guy who bought my cards leave his suitcase containing all my cards and his coin inventory right by the door at the entrance to the room where the show was being held. "I'm going to go get a drink. I'll be right back," I heard him tell someone, and then he just walked out leaving his case just sitting there with some guy who was talking to a girl.

My buddy rejoined me. I said, "If we walked out with that case, our problems would be over." That was all it took. We walked by the case, and my friend picked it up and carried it away as we casually left the hotel. On the drive home we heard a report on the radio: "A gang of thugs stole a suitcase containing a half million dollars worth of valuables from the New York City Coin Show today. The four thieves are described as Hispanic and in their mid-to-late thirties." They obviously didn't have a clue it was us! We were stoked—$500,000! I had gotten a good look at what was in that case—apart from my own few cards and lots of others, there were rolls of gold Krugerands, antique coins, and all kinds of valuables.

My friend and I headed to a couple of coin stores and sold the gold Krugerands for about $50,000, which we split down the middle. I immediately found a new place on the beach to live. A few of my friends moved in, we bought whatever we wanted, and hung out on the beach every day. Life was great!

Since I was a little kid running around the beach scamming the games, I had dreamed of having my own stand on the Boardwalk and looked into getting one. A real estate agent was showing me around, pointing at the various stands. "This one made $300,000 last summer; that one made $250,000." I saw quite a few teenage girls manning the stands, bored out of their minds. I didn't see a lot of customers, and those were the stands that claimed to make the most money.

These figures the agent was quoting seemed very high. There are basically 100 days of summer from Memorial Day to Labor Day. That meant these stands were making $2,500 or $3,000 a day. It didn't seem possible. Most of the games were played with dimes and quarters in those days, but it sounded good. I could see some of the stands had people out there hustling and trying to get the passersby to stop and spend money. I decided what the hell and figured it could be possible. I had the money, and rented a stand in Seaside Heights, New Jersey, for the entire summer at $16,000—paid in advance.

My stand was a dime pitch game. You toss your dime, and if it lands in the Lucky Strike red dot, you win your choice of any prize in the stand. My friends and I manned the booth. For the first few days we were squeaking by with $100 and giving out one huge stuffed animal prize per day. Then we noticed how we had a rush of customers just after someone had won a prize. We refined the game and made it easier. We had a winner every time someone's dime just touched one of the many red dots. Those were called touchers, and we gave away little paper Chinese yo-yos that cost us only two cents each. Every couple of minutes, whenever someone won a two-cent piece of crap, we'd ring the loud winner's bell and attract lots of new customers trying to get the big prizes. Soon we had it down and were making about $1,000 a day.

It was hilarious to see all the little 10- and 12-year-old kids trying to scam me by doing their best to distract me while their friends leaned over to carefully place their dime in the center of the small red dot (those little shits!). Some of them were good, but I was just a few years older than they were and remembered all too well when I was kid performing those tricks.

We did everything to attract people to our game. My buddies and I were the biggest hustlers in the world, and the most we ever made was a little more than $1,000 a day. There was no way these other stands were making anywhere near the $3,000 they claimed. Why the hell would they say they were making so much money when they couldn't possibly be making that much?

As the summer passed I came to learn that all the stands on the Boardwalk the agent had claimed made the most money were owned by the Mob. It all made sense. Those boardwalk stands were the perfect money laundering operation. They staffed the booths with their kids, nephews, and nieces and claimed that they were doing a couple thousand dollars a day. In reality it was maybe $75 or $100, but who's to know? No inventory existed. If they claimed they made $3,000, then they made $3,000, and now that dirty mob money was clean to spend. Most everyone who was a regular on the boardwalk knew all this was Mafia business; the Families were all accepted and respected by everyone. It was a fact of life that I hadn't known, and I didn't care. I was having by far the greatest summer of my life.

I made a quick trip to California to attend a coin show and sold more of the stolen coins all over the state. It made

me over $50,000, plus I learned a lot about dealing with
sleazy self-employed coin dealers along the way. I had two
cars, a nice place, and girls over every night—everything I
could dream of. Of course it was certainly too good to last.

Inevitably the coins got traced back to me via one of
the sales we made to a dealer in New Jersey. One day the
FBI knocked on my door. They'd started an investigation and
asked me where I got the coins. I told them I found the coins
on the beach. They weren't buying it. The next day I was
arrested for "Interstate Travel of Stolen Goods." I bailed out
of jail, and the Feds wanted to know where the rest of the
coins were. I wasn't about to give up anything without a deal.

Two days later I got a phone call from a guy who
called himself Mr. Lou. He sounded like a crude New York
hood. Mr. Lou claimed he worked for the mafia, and said he
wanted the rest of the coins. Since I thought he was an
undercover FBI agent, I told him that I didn't know what he
was talking about and hung up.

The next day my buddy, his girlfriend, and I were
hanging out and working on my car in his garage. All of a
sudden, two guys with stockings on their face burst in with
guns. I first thought it was some friends playing a joke, but
then one of the guys whacked me in the mouth with his gun,
broke my tooth, and ordered us to go to the back room.

One of the guys said, "Let me formally introduce
myself. I'm Mr. Lou, and I don't appreciate the way you
disrespected me when I called you the other day." When my
friend's girlfriend started crying, Mr. Lou told her, "You
know, we may slap around your boyfriend. We may kill your
buddy Tom here, but don't worry honey, we're not going to
touch you."

"What do you want?" I asked with my mouth bleeding.

"Well, here's the deal Tommy," Mr. Lou said as the
other thug whipped out a large pair of wire cutters. "We are
going to ask you where the rest of that half-million-dollar
coin collection is. If you don't tell us, we're going to cut off
your finger. Then we'll ask again. No answer? Another finger
gone 'till there's no more fingers. Then we'll figure out
something else to cut off. Now where are the coins?" he asked
as the other guy placed the wire cutters around my pinky.

"Okay, okay!" I said, not hesitating to answer. "I have the coins hidden at a friend's house. If you can just give me an hour, I can get them for you."

They went outside the room and whispered for a minute. I still didn't know if they were FBI or not, but at that point, I wasn't going to take the chance that I might start losing body parts. They came back and instructed me to get the coins, go back to my place, and wait for their phone call. They also made it clear that if I don't follow their instructions, I would suffer some painful consequences.

I got the remaining coins, which consisted of about a dozen high profile (and probably easily traceable) rare coins worth about $100,000 each, and two dozen low profile coins worth about $10,000 each. When Mr. Lou called, he told me to leave the coins in a phone booth in front of my house, and if everything went down alright, this would be the end of it.

I kept the low profile coins and gave him the more valuable high profile ones, but about an hour later, he called to inform me that he received the coins okay and wanted the rest. "Oh shit!" I yelled into the phone. "I thought you said that once you got these coins it was over!"

"No, we think you have more shit Tommy boy, and we want it all," Mr. Lou said.

I did have those last two dozen coins, but they were not worth nearly as much as the ones I'd just given him, and I knew by now there was no way he'd be happy with what I had left. He'd either get pissed because I'd lied or demand more no matter what I gave him. It was a no-win situation.

I told Mr. Lou that I would check to see if there were anymore coins left behind. I packed my van with as much shit as I could in 15 minutes and started driving as far south as I could and ended up in South Florida. I tried to relax and get my mind off all the shit I'd gotten into in Jersey. It was Spring Break in Florida, and the state was packed with thousands of college kids having fun.

I surprisingly managed to have a good time and met a couple of girls who said they were down from North Florida. I really liked one of the girls, but her friend was wacky. She would stay out all night getting drunk. The girl I liked would get worried, and then the two of us would spend hours looking for her nutty girlfriend. She was always passed out on the beach with a different guy.

One day I said I wanted to drive out to California and start a new life, and the girls begged to come along with me. Before we could get out of Florida, I came down with the worst case of tonsillitis. I had such a high fever I thought my brain was on fire, and my throat hurt so much that I couldn't even swallow water. I made it to a doctor, who prescribed penicillin, and then I went to the drugstore to buy the medication, but that was all I could do. I was so sick and couldn't drive anymore.

I asked the girls if one of them could drive us back, and the crazy girl said, "Sure, I drive!" I didn't know if she could drive or not, but I knew I couldn't so I gave her the wheel. We made it about one block when she clipped the curb on a turn. Immediately a cop pulled us over.

"License and registration," the cop said.

The girl told the cop that she didn't have a license, and the cop asked all three of us to get out of the van. I explained that I was sick, and she had said she could drive us back to the room. The cop asked for everyone's identification, but I was the only one with an I.D. Next the cop took the girls back to his car and spoke to them for about an hour while I was burning up with fever.

Finally the cop came over to me and told me that the girls were 16- and 17-year-old runaways! I was just a kid myself at that time, but it didn't matter. I was over 18 with two runaway girls in my van. The cop threatened to lock me up. The girls had told him of our plan to go to California, and he informed me that if I left Florida with the girls, I would be facing mandatory prison time. After talking to the girls and confirming that they told me they were 18 and 19, he let me go. I had been though a lot of things by that point in my life already, but that was the one incident that made me realize I was not a kid anymore.

Even though the penicillin quickly cured me, I was running low on cash and needed to sell off those last few coins I had. I went off to the nearest coin shop, but by that time the alert was out for me and the coins. I was rearrested and extradited back to New Jersey to be sentenced for the "selling stolen goods" charge. I was told I probably would have received probation, but the fact that I was arrested while out on bail pissed off the judge. He sentenced me to five years at the federal prison in Danbury, Connecticut.

I had certainly had my scrapes with the law before, but this was big time. They told me that under the Youthful Offender Act I would only have to serve a few months and then I'd get out. Before I knew it, I was an inmate in federal prison.

I was very scared at the thought of going to jail, but to tell the truth, this place was nowhere near as scary as I thought it would be. It's just that I had lived my life doing whatever I wanted to do whenever I wanted to do it, but in prison I had to do what THEY wanted me to do whenever THEY wanted me to do it. Every minute of every day I thought about how to get out. I kept waiting and waiting for someone to tell me I would be released. After only five months into my sentence, I felt like years had passed and couldn't stand it anymore.

I was granted a parole hearing and asked only one question, "When do I get out?"

A guy on the parole board responded with another question, "Do you have any more coins?"

"No, absolutely not," I replied, but they didn't believe me. I had been telling them all along that I had no more coins but still kept getting caught with them. That's what had landed me in prison in the first place—lying and continuing to sell coins. They weren't gonna believe me now and said, "We need you to hand over the rest of the collection."

"I told you, I sold it all. I told you exactly where I sold every last piece. There is nothing left to hand over!"

"Because of your continuing lack of cooperation, we recommend continued imprisonment."

Looking back, I know I deserved the sentence that was handed down to me. I did so much shit and probably deserved an even harsher sentence. At that point in my life, I was still a punk who thought I should just get away with every shady thing I did. I sat in prison feeling very sorry for myself. I had counted every minute until that hearing, and when they just shot me down I couldn't believe it. I thought

I was getting out, and here I was looking at the full five years. I was near tears; I could barely call my lawyer. She was sympathetic, but it was something she said that put me over the edge. I had just spent my twenty-second birthday in prison, and my lawyer said to me, "Even in the worst case scenario, if they never grant you parole, you'll only be 26 years old when you get out. That's still so young."

I know now that she was just trying to make me feel better, but when she said, "26 years old when you get out," it sounded like a life sentence. I felt like something or someone was out there waiting for me, but the walls of the prison were keeping me from finding it. I needed to get out, like, NOW! I knew the only way out was to escape, and I also knew they could shoot me dead if I tried and failed. Even so, I decided to put an escape plan in motion and go for it.

I played poker in the television room with some other guys that night and won about $80 worth of postage stamps (inmates used stamps as currency). Back in those days they were 13-cent stamps. I looked at that huge wad of stamps and thought, "Winning these stamps is a sign because I could use these to get money if I could figure a way out of here."

The day after my parole hearing was a foggy Thursday in late December. There was snow on the ground, but it was melting. I waited for the morning bell to ring to signal that all the doors were locked, and I climbed up on a fence that was up against a building wall and got on the roof. The side of the roof I climbed up was only about 12 feet high, but it was a sloped roof. By the time I climbed to the other side, I was about 30 feet in the air. I grabbed onto the edge and hung off, which subtracted about 8 feet from the fall. I hung there for a minute and started to get second thoughts, but I knew there was no turning back. I let go of the edge and fell about 20 feet into a bank of snow.

Just as I jumped, a guard driving a car and carrying a shotgun came around with lights shining all over. I lay hidden in the snow to see how long it would be before he made it back around. It was a long and cold 15 minutes before the headlights came back by. I figured I had 15 minutes, so as soon as he passed by again I got up and ran like hell.

I was prepared, with gloves, long johns, and a jacket. I leapt onto the outer fence and was immediately caught up in barbed wire. My gloves were shredded by razors, but I kept on going. I was so bundled up that the only pain I could feel was in my hands. I made it over the fence and fell heavily on the other side. My two gloves were still stuck in the barbed wire on the prison side.

I ran through the woods for what seemed like forever. I came across a prison guard shooting range that had dummies dressed in the same old army (prison issue) clothes that I was wearing. That scared the shit out of me, and I ran even faster. I could hear cars going by but could not seem to find the highway. Finally I stopped, stood still, and listened. I had been running alongside the highway for at least a mile without realizing it. I changed direction, cut through a bunch of bushes, and found the highway. I also saw a side road that led to a suburban neighborhood. I headed for the smaller road.

It was a few days after Christmas of 1984. As I walked through the neighborhood, I saw an older man shoveling snow from his driveway. I asked him where the nearest post office was, and he replied, "Well, you head down the road a few miles, take a left, then a right...."

Here was another stroke of inexplicable luck: He looked at me and said, "You know, son, I wouldn't mind taking you there if you help me shovel out this driveway." I helped him immediately, and sure enough, he drove me to the post office about five miles away. I was planning to try to sell the many books of postage stamps I had won in the poker game. The post office employee asked me when I got to the counter, "What are you doing? You can't return stamps to the post office for a refund. Sorry."

The guy behind me waiting in line chuckled. "What's the matter son? Your Christmas list was bigger in your mind than in reality?"

"Umm, sure was," I said, "got a few too many stamps here."

"How many you got?"

"I'm not sure, but over $80 worth."

"Tell you what, give me a little discount and I'll buy

them. I'll give you $70 for them." He handed over $70 cash for $82 worth of stamps.

I walked to the bus station and jumped on a bus for Bayonne where one of my close friends lived. My friend was driving the classic Firebird I had when I was sentenced to prison. He was surprised to see me, to say the least, but he paid me the money he owed me for the car. Now I had some cash. We drove into New York and bought some phony I.D. in Times Square in the name of Tom Rizzo—pretty close to my real name of Tom Riccio. We tried to sneak into Studio 54, the hottest place in town at the time, but couldn't get in.

It was New Year's Eve, and we watched the ball drop. Afterwards we wandered over to a bench and talked for a while. It was now 1985. I hoped it would be a better year than the last one. My friend asked, "What are you going to do? You can't stay around here."

I thought for a second while shivering in the freezing cold New York City air. "I'm going to California or Florida, somewhere warm." I always liked those two states.

We drove to the Newark airport in New Jersey. The first flight out was at 6:00 a.m. to Los Angeles, California. I bought my ticket, thanked my friend for his help, and boarded the plane. I had a strong feeling that something better had to be waiting for me on the other side.

Chapter Six

LOS ANGELES/TRUE LOVE
1985

I landed in Los Angeles five hours later. It was like landing on another planet. I felt like Dorothy must've felt when she landed in Oz. The skies were blue, the sun was shining, and it was an even 80 degrees. It had been about zero in New Jersey. *Man, my life is really gonna change now*, I thought as I stood outside the airport. *Everything is gonna be all right.*

I wound up renting a little place by the week in Hollywood. I crossed Hollywood Boulevard my first day in the new place to buy a sandwich at a little deli, and a cop stopped me for jaywalking. He actually wrote me—or Thomas Rizzo according to my I.D.—a jaywalking ticket. As soon as he turned his back, I ripped the ticket into shreds and threw it up in the air. It was ridiculous.

I found a job working at a baseball card shop in the heart of Hollywood. Baseball cards were just starting to become a big business, and I knew baseball cards inside out. The first week all I did was help the owner sort cards. Then he let me follow up with customers who wanted to buy and sell certain cards or collections. I started to get a feel for what was popular and what was valuable. I had always been pretty good at making deals with people: buying and selling. The owner of the shop really liked me because I made him a lot of cash.

As soon as I put some money together, I bought a used car, a little Vega that barely ran because it stalled so often. I then went to the DMV to get a California driver's license. The car kept stalling during my test, and I was sweating it. I was sure they wouldn't give me a license, but at the end of the test the examiner turned to me and said, "Anyone who can get through the driver's test in this piece of shit deserves two licenses." He passed me, and I got an official California driver's license in the name of Tom Rizzo. I was all set. I had a job, an apartment, and a Vega that needed two quarts of oil with every tank of gas. The car was equipped with a CB radio and PA horn. I added a nice stereo and a high-powered spotlight. One day I went to the Burger King on Hollywood Boulevard, and as I walked in, I noticed a couple of guys talking to a VW Beetle full of girls. One of the girls in the back seat was absolutely gorgeous, and I couldn't take my eyes off her. She was just the kind of beautiful California girl I had always dreamed of. I kicked myself the whole time I was inside eating my hamburger, thinking I should have found some way to talk to her or get a number—anything.

When I came back outside, the guys were still there talking to the girls. I jumped into my car, got on my PA, and announced that no loitering was permitted in the parking lot in a very cop-like tone. The guys jumped back and said, "Okay, okay." As soon as they were gone, one of the girls came running over to me. "Hey, those guys offered us drugs and tried to make us come with them to some party."

"Look, I'm not a cop," I told the girl. "I just wanted to meet your friend."

"That's my sister, Irene," she told me. We walked back to the VW and talked. The gorgeous girl in the back seat was also very friendly. The girls explained to me that they were looking for Cyndi Lauper tickets.

"Oh, I've got tickets to that show," I lied. "Give me your number and we'll go."

"Really?" they squealed. Irene's sister wrote down a number. I later discovered the Cyndi Lauper show wasn't for another couple of months. I couldn't wait that long to see Irene again and went to a ticket agency to buy some Prince tickets, then gave her a call. I wound up having to take both Irene and her sister to the show, but we all had a great time. I fell in love with Irene almost immediately.

Irene was 18 years old and had just gotten a job after graduating from high school. She didn't drink or smoke, didn't do drugs, and was as sweet as could be. She didn't have a bad word to say about anything or anybody. As I got to know her better, I couldn't believe how kind and easygoing she was. I managed to escape from prison for a reason, and now I knew that reason was Irene.

After five months of steady dating, I knew things between us couldn't go any further until I told her the truth about my situation. I explained to her how I had some very serious issues and told her a little about the stolen coins. "Well, it sounds like you had some problems, but you seem to be out of them now," she said.

"Not really, I'm still kind of in the middle of them. I escaped from federal prison."

She couldn't quite believe it and after a long pause asked, "What are you going to do?"

"I don't know. I want to clear this up and put this behind me, but I don't want to leave you."

We talked for a while, and Irene finally said, "Well, whatever's going to happen will happen, but I'll be behind you."

Irene had very strict parents and had to be home by 1:00 a.m., no exceptions. I was speeding her home one night and ran a red light. A cop stopped me and went to write me a ticket. He returned to my window and said, "We have a bit of a problem, Mr. Rizzo. You got a jaywalking ticket five or six months ago."

"Oh, yeah," I had forgotten all about it.

"Well, that turned into a warrant for $170."

That was a bummer, but I had some money. "Okay, I'll pay it right now."

"No, no, you have to go to the jailhouse and pay it there."

The cop took me to the jail where they fingerprinted me. Things didn't move as fast back in 1985 without computers and the Internet. I paid the bond and was just walking out when a clerk came out from the back office and said, "Wait a minute...Rizzo, Riccio.... What's going on here? You're not going anywhere. The Feds want to talk to you!"

Irene visits me in prison at Terminal Island in 1985, after they caught me on escape.

I was taken into custody and placed at Terminal Island. Irene came out to see me and swore, "I'll wait as long as it takes." I was now facing a lot more time than my original sentence because of the escape. The judge who heard my case was rumored to be very tough, and I had a young and inexperienced lawyer who annoyed him at our first hearing. The judge asked for a plea, and my lawyer said, "Not Guilty."

The judge got upset and asked me, "Son, are you Thomas Riccio?"

"Yes, I am," I replied.

"And aren't you supposed to be serving your sentence across the country in Danbury Federal prison?" he asked

"Yes," I confirmed.

"Then why in the world wouldn't you want to plead guilty? I can sentence you now, and you can get back to serving your time."

My lawyer jumped in, "Well, your honor, we don't know the details of how he got out. It may not be escape. Maybe someone took him out by force, against his will. We just don't know yet, so we want to plead 'Not Guilty' for now."

The judge seemed pissed, but it turned out for the best, because it gave us time to get letters to the court. Irene wrote a nice letter to the judge and so did the owner of the card shop where I worked. My family back east all wrote pleading for leniency as well.

At my sentencing the judge told me, "You have a lot of people standing behind you who really care for you. It appears that you were living a clean life here in California while you were on your breakout, so here's what I'm going to do: I'm supposed to give you five years, minimum, for escape. I am going to sentence you to those five years, but the first six months will be in a halfway house, and the rest can be served on probation." I wound up only getting sentenced to six extra months for escaping—just about the same amount of time I'd been out. I was very lucky.

Even though I was caught, I still believed the real reason I had made it over that wall was to meet Irene, the woman I should marry. I proposed, and she accepted before I left to serve my time in a high-security prison in Terre Haute, Indiana. My life now had a purpose. I had Irene waiting for me, and that made it all worth it.

Chapter Seven

TERRE HAUTE/BASTROP
1985-1988

Level One federal prison is a camp. This is where you find the rich white-collar inmates who are in for tax fraud and other offenses like that. It's the kind of institution you hear about where middle-aged fat guys show up, serve a few months, and then end up coming out thinner, in shape from exercising, and looking like they have been at a health camp. It has no walls and inmates can work outside the prison and easily run away, if they want to.

Level Two also has people from the upper income and society levels; generally the inmates are those who have been in prison serving a long sentence and have been moved down to a Level Two as they prepare to leave the system. Even though inmates are contained within walls, very little violence occurs at a Level Two institution.

Level Three federal prisons start to get crazy. It has a wall surrounding it with barbed wire on top.

Level Four is for inmates doing life and habitually dangerous and violent offenders. The institution is walled and has guard towers with guns. Guards are supervising inmates all the time.

Level Five used to be Alcatraz until it got shut down. The penitentiary at Marion, Illinois, is a Level Five prison. It houses hardcore out-of-control prisoners from all over the country. They're the worst of the worst. They're so bad the states won't even deal with them in the state system. It's the kind of place where the inmates are locked down nearly 23 hours a day and even wear shackles to the shower. A guard with a gun watches them every minute. It's pretty hard to be assigned right off to a Level Five prison. You usually wind up there for killing a prison guard or something like that. You have to "earn" your way into a Level Five institution because it's for the baddest of the bad.

When I was captured after my escape, I was classified as a Level Four and sentenced to a facility in Indiana. Most of the other inmates in the Terre Haute prison were serving sentences like triple life; I was the only one with a five-year sentence. Very soon after I got there, a guy robbed all the stuff out of my cell. He didn't even try to hide it and threw in some advice while he was at it, "Go tell the guards that your cell got robbed. Tell them your life was threatened. A young kid like you, serving only five years with all these lifers, you're going to have big problems in here. This is not for you. I'd roll it up fast if I were you."

"Roll it up" meant get your clothes, roll them all up in your blanket, tell the guards your life was threatened, and get the hell out.

I soon discovered lots of Native Americans were serving time in federal prisons. One of them was my cellmate while I was waiting to be reclassified. He was a quiet little guy who constantly rolled cigarettes. They used to hand out tobacco to inmates in those days. This guy rolled cigarettes night and day. I'd be lying in the bottom bunk at night trying to sleep, and tobacco would rain down on my face because he'd be up there rolling more smokes. "Hey Chief," I said one night. "Do you mind doing that down here?"

That was all it took. The man went crazy, leaped off the bed, and started punching me. I managed to get him in a headlock, but then he bit me. I couldn't believe it. The guards eventually showed up and separated us. I wound up getting charged with fighting and got even more time added onto my sentence for this violation of the rules.

Finally they reclassified me, and I was able to get transferred to a lower-level prison in Texas because I had no violence on my record. One of the men I did time with in Texas helped me get my time back when we discovered that the little Indian guy who bit me was officially criminally insane. He'd had quite a few incidents over the years.

Texas was a much more manageable environment. Meanwhile Irene lived with her parents in L.A., worked her job, and waited for me.

One day while I was locked up, Irene was walking to work when a limo drove up. The window came down, and the guy invited Irene into his limo and offered to take her anywhere she wanted to go. Irene was sure she recognized the guy, and when he opened his mouth it left no doubt. It was Bruce Springsteen! She turned him down and told several people what had happened. Most people at her workplace thought she was mistaken, but then on the afternoon news there was a story about Bruce Springsteen being in town to speak at a union meeting. He was wearing the same outfit as the one he wore in the limo earlier that day when he tried to pick up Irene.

I thought it was pretty cool that Irene turned down a date with "The Boss" in his prime because she was waiting for me. I couldn't wait to get out and show her I was worth the wait.

Irene sent me this pin-up picture of her to cheer me up while I was in prison in 1986. This was about the time when Bruce Springsteen tried to pick her up.

Chapter Eight

SAN BERNARDINO CARD SHOW 1988 - 1989

Thanks to good behavior, I got out of prison in less than three years. As soon as I got released, my brother Paul bought my entire baseball card collection. I hated to sell it but needed money to get back on my feet. He said, "I'll give you $5,000 now and $5,000 more at Christmas." I accepted the $5,000, rented an apartment in Los Angeles, and bought my dream car—a '69 Camaro for $1,900. I slowly worked on it by fixing it up, getting a new paint job, and tinkering with the engine.

Irene's parents had a fit when I started seeing her again. "We never believed you'd do this—wait around for some convict. Whatever you do, don't marry this guy. He's a convict!" They never stopped. I also had to bring her home by whatever arbitrary deadline her father set. She was 21 years old by this time, not a kid.

Irene's father had quite a temper; he used to yell at her, "You keep the hours of a two-bit whore!" and all kinds of other remarks. I didn't like hearing him speak to his daughter that way.

"We are adults now," I told Irene. "It's no one's business where we are or what we're doing together. I don't want to hear your father ranting and raving anymore. I proposed and because of his objections we didn't get married a long time ago! I won't live like this anymore." As much as I loved her and was thankful she had waited for me, I could not handle this situation anymore.

Irene grabbed a trash bag and started filling it up with her stuff. Her father was shocked and couldn't believe it. She came with me and got pregnant about a month later. I could not have been happier. I felt ready to start a family and knew Irene would make a great mom. None of the girlfriends I'd had before had been anything close to my idea of what a mother should be. Irene was! She was the California girl I always dreamed of having.

One day shortly after Irene arrived, I came out of our crappy little neighborhood apartment/hotel room that we rented by the week to discover my car was gone. Stolen! My brother owed me the final payment of $5,000 in a few months. I called him and explained my problem. He said, "Tell you what, I'll give you $4,000 right now, but that's all you get since I don't owe it for another three months; or else you can wait and I'll pay the whole amount when I owe it to you."

I told Irene, "Look, I have a few hundred dollars. We can go to Vegas, and I can try to win the money for another car, or I can take the money my brother owes me now but lose $1,000. If I don't win, I could always take the deal for less when we get back. I think it makes sense to go to Vegas and try to win."

Irene was never into gambling or Las Vegas, but she agreed to go. As soon as I got into the casino, I placed parlay bets immediately. A parlay ticket pays several times your money, but you have to win all your bets to win the parlay. The more bets you have on a ticket, the more money you win. When I woke up the next morning, I saw that eight out of nine of my games had won including several long shot parlays. One was a seven-team parlay that paid about 100 to 1. I was up about $10,000!

I was having a good day and wanted to make it even better, so once again I asked Irene to marry me. This time she said "Yes!" We both agreed we didn't care for a big expensive wedding complete with judgmental relatives. We just wanted a simple private ceremony, and Las Vegas was the perfect place for it. We went to this little place off the strip called San Francisco Sally's, an Old West-themed wedding chapel. They provided everything: a beautiful old-fashioned wedding dress for Irene, a classy tuxedo for me, nice photographs, and even a video of the whole ceremony. The whole thing cost a grand total of $350! After the ceremony

Irene and I get married in an old-fashioned style Las Vegas Chapel on January 9th, 1989.

we had a great meal, and then spent our honeymoon night in a nicer room at the Stardust Hotel. In the morning we went straight home to L.A.

Posted on our door when we got back was a note from the Montebello Police Department saying they had recovered my car. It was just some kids out joyriding, and nothing was wrong with the vehicle. The week started off bad when my car was stolen, but it ended up as one of my better weeks when I won over $10,000, finally got married to Irene, and had my classic car returned.

Life ran smoothly from that point on. My brother let me use the cards he bought from me to start a business selling at baseball card shows, and we were doing quite well. New baseball cards were becoming popular, and my brother Paul had a vintage card collection. Basketball, hockey, football cards...those markets were all exploding at the time. I was trading old cards for new cards.

In 1989 a Billy Ripken card was published. As a joke, the batboy had written "Fuck Face" on the bottom of the bat pictured on the Fleer rookie card of Cal Ripken's little brother, and you could clearly read it. The card company realized their error pretty quickly and blacked it out on most editions, but some of the first cases got out to the public. This card was an absolute phenomenon. It was kind of strange to see ten-year-old kids asking, "Do you have the Fuck Face Ripken card?" They were selling for $150 each.

One guy I knew owned two of these cards and was willing to trade them for a Whitey Ford card, which would normally sell for about $100. Done deal! My brother scrutinized the deal at the end of the day and was furious. "You traded a Whitey Ford card for two Fuck Face cards? You're the Fuck Face!"

I could see his point. The new cards were fads that came and went while something like a Whitey Ford card would always hold its value, but at that moment in time, it had been a smart deal. He just couldn't understand it, and I thought it was time to move on.

"Listen Paul, I can't take this anymore. You don't understand how the business is working now." It was my job to make money trading and dealing cards, but he criticized every move I made. I had enough! I sent him all his cards back and went into business for myself with the small amount of money I'd saved.

The next weekend, I was working for myself and trying to find a good deal on a collection at a Burbank card show when I met this old guy who started talking about the business. "You know, I own a gift and candy shop in the Beverly Center mall just outside Beverly Hills. We sell movie posters and stuff like that. It's right outside the movie theaters. I don't know anything about the sports card business, but people come in every day asking for baseball cards. If you want, I'll let you rent some space in my shop, cheap: $500 a month. You could put a couple showcases in there. It might be a good move for both of us."

I approached an acquaintance, a guy named Robbie who looked just like Richard Marx (a pop star at the time). I used to see him at every show where I was dealing cards for my brother. He and I sold similar types of cards, and I thought we'd make a good team. I said, "Look, this guy offered me the opportunity to deal baseball cards out of the Beverly Center."

"Oh my God, that's the ritziest mall in the city. I live in Hollywood, not far from there. I'd love to do this with you."

"Well then, let's be partners. I need stock because I gave all my stock back to my brother just yesterday."

"You gave all that back? Well, what are you going in with?"

"Oh, I'll make deals in the shop. Don't worry, within six months I'll match your inventory."

"Hmm, okay, well, do you have any money for showcases?"

"Not really, I just paid rent and my wife is pregnant...."

"Let me get this straight. You have nothing, but want me to be your partner? Look, I love that location. Let me just give you a few hundred bucks for the location."

"No way, I'm keeping that location."

"How are you going to run a baseball card shop without any cards?"

"We're gonna use your stuff at first. I'll build up a collection again, trust me."

"Let me think about this," he said, and walked away shaking his head. A day or so later he called me on the phone.

"I'll give you a thousand dollars for that Beverly Center location!"

"Let's get this straight. I want that location, and I am going to figure out a way to do this. With or without you, I will make this happen."

"I want to do it too, and I know you'd be a good partner, but you have nothing! Can't you call your brother up and grovel a little bit? Have him return some of his stuff, so we can at least start on an even playing field? You can't even buy showcases!"

"I will very soon. I will figure something out."

"Okay," he sighed. "Come to the San Bernardino show and we'll talk some more about it."

As I walked into the San Bernardino card show, I saw a young guy with a small shoebox full of cards. I stopped to take a look. He had a Nolan Ryan rookie card, hot at the time, a Tom Seaver rookie card, and a couple other interesting cards—probably a couple thousand dollars worth of stuff in there. I asked him what he wanted for the whole box; he said $1,000. Not a bad deal, but I had to ask, "Do you have any more cards?"

"I have an entire storage room full of cards. I don't want to keep paying rent for the storage; I want to clear it out," he said. "I'd like to get rid of them all in one deal." I accompanied the guy to his storage, which was packed with box after box of cards (5,000 cards in each box). He also had dozens of binders with all the popular new stuff of that time—Jose Canseco, Daryl Strawberry, the new superstar rookie cards, complete sets, and everything else. These cards were liquid cash!

"Why are you getting rid of all this in such a hurry?" I asked.

"I had an inheritance a few years ago, and I spent most of my money on these cards. I'm just not into them anymore, and I'm leaving to go to college in Northern California. I need some extra money for school, and I have to get rid of the storage space."

"How much do you want for everything?" I asked the kid.

"You tell me. Make me an offer."

"A thousand dollars for everything," I said.

"No way! If I can't get $2,000 for everything then forget it. I'll hold on to it and deal with all this next summer when I get done with the school year." I wasn't sure what the situation really was, because this collection was worth at least $50,000. He had to be aware of some of its value, but when it came down to it, I didn't need to know. He was willing to sell, and I was more than willing to buy.

"Done deal! Two thousand dollars." Unfortunately I had no money. I did have a '69 Camaro, which couldn't hold all the boxes and binders. I loaded all the highly valuable stuff in my car, and then we loaded the other boxes into the kid's truck—not quite the pure gold that the newer rookie cards were but still valuable stuff. We headed for the show again, and I assured the guy that I had his money there.

I ran into the show floor, grabbed a dolly from a dealer I knew, and started wheeling in just the boxes full of common cards and comic books. I hadn't gotten 100 feet into the show before I was surrounded by about 4 dealers asking, "Hey Tom, what have you got there?" They started looking through the boxes. One box held 30 to 40 cards of a player named Cecil Fielder, who was very hot at the time—each card was worth about $30 each. Howard Johnson had a breakout year, and a bunch of his cards were just tossed into the common box. One of the guys spotted a box of 1950s commons and said, "Okay Tom, what do you want for the entire collection on this dolly?"

"Thirty-five hundred dollars!" I replied.

"If you're willing let it go for thirty-three hundred and take a check for part of it, I'll take it right now."

"Done deal," I said. I knew this dealer's check would be good. He gave me $1,300 cash and wrote me a check for $2,000. Meanwhile the college kid was sitting in the snack bar getting antsy. I told him that I had to cash a check. I showed him the check and he looked at it. "I know that guy; I've been to his card shop. I'll take that check." So I signed it over to him. He took it and went on his way. I had $1,300 in cash and a huge new inventory in my car. I was really stoked!

I went over to Robbie's table, and before I could say anything, he said, "I've been thinking about this Tom, and I just don't think we're the right match. We deal in the same kind of stuff and you don't have any inventory."

"What if I had all the newest, latest, hottest sellers?" I responded.

"Well, that would be a different story, but you don't."

"Come with me," I said and took him out to my car where he examined the boxes and binders full of cards.

"What did you do, rob a card shop?"

"Nah, I just did a deal."

"In the two hours you were here you did this deal? I can't believe it. You are the luckiest guy in the world. If you match my stuff dollar for dollar with this kind of inventory, we'll be partners."

I was going to do everything I could to make this new opportunity very successful.

Chapter Nine

BEVERLY CENTER MALL/LOTTERY 1989

The shop owner Bill was spending $15,000 a month for his prime location in the Beverly Center mall. My new partner and I paid him only $500 a month for a small space for our two showcases in his store. As we were setting up the displays on our first day, customers were already trying to buy our stuff. By the end of the week, our little section was doing more business than his entire shop. Lots of Hollywood actor kids and adults used to come in to see what we had and buy expensive cards—and they paid the retail price. We were making money hand over fist.

Robbie, my partner, had family and friends in Chicago, and whenever a family problem came up he'd run home for days at a time to deal with it. Meanwhile I was making $2,000 a day profit at the shop and sending him half the money. "Listen," I told him, "when you get back I need to take some time off. I want to go on vacation with my wife. She's pregnant, I've been working constantly, I need a break, and you need to handle some of this."

Robbie agreed. When he came home from his latest trip, he was supposed to take over at the shop but didn't show up. Customers were at the store wanting to buy things from us, but no one was there to sell it to them. The owner would call, and I would have to rush in. Later Robbie explained to me that he had a hot date the night before and couldn't make it in. Then he picked a fight with me about my clothing style, saying I dressed more like Fred Flintstone than a dealer in the Beverly Center. I have never been the best dresser in the world, that's for sure, but I didn't think it was relevant. My partner, on the other hand, fit right in at the Beverly Center. He was always decked out in the latest 80s style punk clothes. However, he certainly wasn't complaining about all the money I made every time he was gone.

Most of our customers preferred to deal with me, no matter how I was dressed. I had plenty of contacts, and everybody in the business wanted to make deals with me. Robbie could never manage to show up on time. I was getting very tired of the situation, to the point we were arguing with each other at the shop. The owner intervened, "Look, you two need to come to a decision. I can't have you arguing with each other in front of customers. One of you needs to go."

Unfortunately for me, Bill was gay, fashionable, and had a crush on my partner. Robbie had a secret meeting with Bill, and I could see the writing on the wall. Bill said to me, "Make a fair deal with Robbie; he probably fits in here a little better." I guess I wasn't his type.

"Wait a minute! I founded this place, it was my idea. I've made it a success and put in all the hours—he's hardly here!"

"Yes, but this situation isn't working with the two of you fighting. The both of you together just doesn't work."

I told my wife that at Bill's insistence, I was meeting with Robbie to see if we could make a deal to buy me out of the business. Irene came with me into the shop and started yelling at my partner, very unusual for her. "My husband built this place. He's here working every day, and now that it's successful you want to steal it from him!"

"Look I'm going to be fair," Robbie said. "I'll pay for your showcases. I'll give you a couple thousand dollars in inventory."

We each had at least $15,000 apiece in inventory in that shop. "I want $10,000 and all of the inventory that's in our shop."

"No way! I could just throw you out!"

"No you can't, the phone's in my name.... I could throw you out. Bill can't even throw me out. This business is in my name. Go check out renters and tenancy laws if you don't believe me."

He didn't believe me and found out I was right. He came back to me and said, "Five thousand dollars and all the inventory that's in the showcases right now, but you'll have to give me time to come up with the five thousand dollars."

I said, "Okay, Robbie, fine. I'll take it, let's just settle this." He boxed up the inventory for me, and my wife and I left. Irene was crying her heart out. "I can't believe it. You finally got a good business going, and he stole it. I'm pregnant. What are we going to do?" She was highly upset. So was I, but I didn't want to worry her even more. "We'll be okay," I assured her.

We stopped at the store on our way home to buy some groceries, and I bought a bunch of lottery tickets. I had a very strong premonition that I would win, but Irene seemed upset. "You just lost your business! Why are you throwing more money away? We have a baby coming in case you've forgotten? Are you crazy?"

"I know hon, but I really feel like I'm gonna win. I have a feeling." She was not convinced.

Our company had contracted to do a show the next day, but that was no longer my problem. I woke up in the middle of that night with a thought: *Hmm.... I have all this inventory. I'm the one who made all the plans and arrangements for the show this morning. I'm going to that fucking show myself!*

"Don't even worry," I told my wife as I shoved everything I owned into my '69 Camaro: boxes full of cards, table display cases, a dolly, you name it. I was completely loaded down. "We're gonna be all right, I promise," I said as I drove off. Irene looked unconvinced.

I still had that premonition and stopped by 7-Eleven to buy a hot cocoa and five lotto quick-picks. I had the best show of my life that day. I made $12,000 on a stack of Ken Griffey Jr. rookie cards that were "back-doored" from Upper Deck. That was the hottest card at the time, and executives at Upper Deck were printing them like money. I was selling them as fast as I got them. It was all about finding them, and that day I was in the right place at the right time when I bought an 800-count box from some guy who worked at the factory. It was one of my unexplainable lucky days, and the day was still young.

A tense moment occurred when Robbie, my former partner, showed up (late again of course), but I had always made all the show arrangements for our company and the guy running the show knew me. He gave Robbie his own separate booth in the back of the Shrine Auditorium.

Robbie was cursing up a storm. I had secured a prime location by signing up early, and he was stuck in a dark back corner with no traffic. That booth space was the key to my success that day. Robbie and I both knew it.

I got home late. It had been a long day, but I was very happy with the money I made. My pockets were stuffed with bills. As I was laying all the money out and sorting through the bills, I saw the lottery ticket I bought that morning. I never even bothered to check the winning numbers. How many people do? But I still had that funny nagging feeling.

I called the phone number to check the winning numbers and wrote down each number as the automated voice read them off. I couldn't believe it and checked the numbers again—they were a match. I told my wife, and at first she thought I was joking, but when I called the 7-Eleven to check the prize amount, she knew it was the real deal. I asked how much I won, and the clerk said "The final amount won't come out 'till 6:00 a.m., but from past results, I can tell you that 5 out of 6 plus the bonus number wins about $100,000."

I couldn't sleep all night. At 6:00 a.m. the official lottery results came in. Irene and I drove to a store to pick up the official ticket with the final results. I ran in, got them, and then raced back to the car to sit and read the results with Irene. I placed my finger over the number and slowly revealed the winning figure. I was hoping to see a 1 for $100,000, but the first number I saw was a 7. It appeared that we had won $75,500. We looked up and saw the manager of the store standing by the window smiling, giving us the thumbs-up sign. I walked in and said, "I was hoping to win $100,000, but $75,500 is great."

The guy looked puzzled, "$75,000? Buddy, you won $755,000!"

CALIFORNIA
MON JUL10 89

WINNING NUMBERS
LOTTO
SAT JUL 8 89
21 38 41 42 48 49
BONUS NUMBER: 02
NO 6/6 WINNER
6/6 $ .00
2 5/6+$ 755355.00
200 5/6 $ 3891.00
11138 4/6 $ 63.00
211171 3/6 $ 5.00
NOT   FOR   SALE

This is the actual ticket I picked up at 7-Eleven the morning after I won the lottery and discovered that I won over three quarters of a million dollars.

"Get out of here!" I looked at the ticket again. The 7, the 5, another 5, the 0s.... I counted again. It was $755,000! Irene and I were ecstatic, to say the least. "What are you going to do now?" the store owner asked me.

First I went straight to the lottery office in Whittier, California. We were all excited when we walked in with the ticket, but then some special lottery investigators started interrogating me: "Did you buy this ticket or get it from someone else?"

"I bought it myself," I said.

"Exactly what day and time did you buy the ticket? Did you buy anything else with the ticket? Who was working when you bought the ticket?"

I felt like I was being questioned for a crime, but then they said, "Congratulations! Don't take those questions personally. We ask all winners those same questions to verify the ticket is in fact theirs." They gave me a receipt and said a check would arrive in about three weeks.

Then I drove directly to the Shrine Auditorium where Robbie was setting up his booth in the back. He was not happy to see me, and I said, "Robbie, about that $5,000 you owe me, I'll take it in cards." I knew just what I was going to do—start my own trading card business. I picked out a bunch of high-end cards, and he started to nickel and dime me on the prices. "Be nice Robbie, I'm giving you a big break," I told him.

"Yeah, why are you doing this?" he asked suspiciously.

"I'm gonna open my own store," I told him.

"Yeah right! With what? Did you win the lottery or something?" Robbie said sarcastically.

"As a matter of fact, yes I did."

Thomas J. Riccio

"You son-of-a-bitch, you did not."

"Oh yeah, I won the lottery!" I showed him the results card. "Thanks for the cards, we're straight now." Then I left.

This is my actual check I received from the California State lottery office. I thought this money was the last gift from God I would ever need, but within a few years I was back on the prayer hotline once again.

Chapter Ten

BUENA PARK
1989

My life seems to be a series of extreme highs and lows. I realize that not everyone had the luck and opportunities I've been blessed with, but I also don't know of anyone who has hit rock bottom as often as me. I've come to know that I can get past those lows as long as I have my health and my freedom. If you don't give up, the highs will come back around the corner. That's pretty much my life.

I was riding a huge high. I had just won the lottery! I gave everyone in my family and Irene's cash presents. The in-laws wanted loans, but of course, they never paid me back. I also took care of some personal debts.

Once the gift-giving was done I took the rest of my lottery money and bought a house in the suburb of Buena Park with a mini-mall in front of it. The mini-mall had space for my baseball card shop named New and Classic Baseball Cards, my wholesale office, and some extra units for tenants.

I opened my shop by having some rookies from the California Angels and Los Angeles Dodgers sign autographs at my store. I even had cheerleaders from the Los Angeles Raiders come by to take photos with my customers. My mini-mall and the celebrity signings were a great success.

One of the tenants in my shopping center was a nice older Latino guy named Alan who had a great family that worked with him in his custom tailoring store. One day I hosted a personal appearance for Lee Stevens, a rookie with the California Angels, at my shop. There was a big crowd when Stevens showed up and signed cards for fans. The next day Alan came to my shop and said, "Tom, I have a nephew who's a boxer. He's 17 years old. He's won the Golden Gloves and all kinds of awards. He's getting very famous in the Latino community—they call him 'The Golden Boy.' Maybe he could come and do a signing at your shop. He'd bring a lot of fans."

I'd never heard of him. Allen pulled out a picture of his nephew to show me. He looked like a nice little kid, but not like any boxer I'd ever seen before. I said, "I just don't do much with boxers. Baseball is really my sport, sorry." I wanted to be nice; I liked the man. He continued to talk about his nephew to me every time I saw him, and I continued to make excuses.

One day I saw Alan with his nephew playing basketball in the back parking lot. "Tom, Tom, come over, I want to introduce you to my nephew!" I went over and shook the kid's hand. He didn't look a day over 14 years old and had a big smile. He was a very good-looking kid, but he still didn't look like a boxer to me. "I saw your shop, it's really cool. You know I could sign photos for you if you wanted," the kid said.

I did not want to hurt this family's feelings. I didn't want to embarrass anybody, especially the kid. "I appreciate your offer; it's just that I don't really have many boxing fans."

"Oh sure, I understand," he said. He came by the shop later and bought a few cards, no hard feelings—a super-nice kid.

A year or so later, this pretty-boy-boxer was in the Olympics and won the Gold Medal! His smiling face was everywhere: Oscar de la Hoya, The Golden Boy! I couldn't get away from his image. This was the kid I'd turned away, more than once. I went back to his uncle. "That nephew of yours, Oscar, I'll let him sign at my shop."

He laughed. "Tom, Oscar has four agents now. He's doing commercials and everything else. He doesn't have time to talk to me anymore, but I appreciate it." I really missed the boat on that one.

*   *   *

Home computers were just starting to get big at the time. There was a new service called the SportsNet where a select group of dealers nationwide could log on via satellite back in those days before the Internet. SportsNet was a computer service for dealers only, a subscription service that cost something like $300 a month. It had a yellow/orange screen with numbers going across. This was how dealers kept in contact, buying and selling products to each other.

Card shops were popping up everywhere. The competition was so brutal that I decided rather than just run my own store I would wholesale cases of cards from SportsNet to the card shops in a very big way. My winnings helped me jump in big instead of starting small and growing. The business boomed beyond my expectations. It was amazing! I would buy 20 cases of new card product from a dealer in Philadelphia for $1,000 a case, have that dealer drop-ship them (with my labels) to Seattle for $2,000 a case, and make a quick $20,000 without ever even laying my hands on the cards or touching the product. I would send the dealer in Philly a check for $20,000, and the dealer in Seattle would send me a check for $40,000. I was doing deals like that every week. Business was great, and I managed to keep it going and growing.

On September 14, 1989, after a long night of labor, Irene finally gave birth to our first daughter, Angela Marie Riccio, by C-section.

*　　　*　　　*

I had a great friend from New Jersey who had been calling me for months telling me that his wife had gone crazy and left him. Richie was hurting; he wanted to divorce her but didn't have enough money. I told him, "Come on out here for a break. We'll go to Vegas and bet on the World Series. We'll win some money, and you can pay for your divorce." The Oakland A's had a great team that year. They were playing the San Francisco Giants in a Bay Area Series, and I had a strong feeling that the A's would win. If they didn't, I was going to make sure he left with money even if I had to give it to him. I hoped some of my recent luck would rub off on him.

On my way to Vegas I heard the high-pitched noise of the Emergency Broadcast System come on the radio, announcing an earthquake in San Francisco right before the start of the World Series. They wound up postponing the game, and there I was in Vegas with no World Series to bet on.

At that time of year, football games were played on the weekend. It was now a Thursday. No basketball in October, so all there was to bet on was hockey, which I knew nothing about. I was sitting in the sports book with my friend, pondering my options, and a guy told me that the new hockey team named the Ottawa Senators couldn't score to save their lives, but they had a good defense and didn't give up too many goals. They usually lost every game 1-0, 2-0, or maybe 2-1. The over/under (total score bet) was low, five and a half but not low enough. "Bet all the money you've got on the under in the Ottawa Senators game," he advised me. "It's a lock."

I took the $10,000 I brought with me, and bet that the score of the Senators game would be less than five and a half total goals and won! It was a 2-0 game. I didn't want to keep betting on hockey because I knew nothing about the sport. So, I decided to wait until the pro football games on Sunday.

On Friday night, my friend and I were having a great time. We stopped by the Hilton sports book and wound up listening to a live radio show where three experts were analyzing all the college football games that were coming up. The three men on the panel gave their picks for every single college game for the next day, all 52 games. I didn't follow college games too closely, so I thought I'd watch and listen to the live show.

"I think Notre Dame is going to cover the spread," one would say.

"I don't think so. They're not even going to win," another old guy would say.

"I like the under in the Michigan game," the other guy would announce. I started paying attention, and out of the hours of debating, there were only six different bets that all three of them agreed on. I took the money I won on the hockey game and bet on those six picks with a few different parlay tickets and went to bed. When I woke up, I turned on the TV and saw that I'd won every bet except for one game that was still going on. I went down to the sports book to watch.

The game I needed was not on the big screen TV, but I watched the updates on the sports book ticker tape. The last update said my team was winning by four points, but the other team was driving with less than two minutes to go. Even if I lost, I would still win a few grand from betting on one four-team parlay and one five-team parlay. But if I won the last game, I would win ALL my parlays—at least $100,000. Only a couple minutes were left in the game, but the final score did not come across the ticker for about a half hour. Finally they posted the results: Ohio State won, and more importantly, they covered the three-point spread. I had won all six bets—every parlay ticket had won! I turned to my friend Richie and said, "I can't believe this, all my parlay tickets are winners!"

I went up to the counter and said, "Account number 172, how much did I win?"

The woman behind the cage wouldn't tell me. She took my I.D. and did a bunch of stuff but refused to tell me what I'd won. I was getting very pissed because I didn't have a printed ticket with my bet. It was all done on my account. I was afraid they were going to screw with me.

Finally the sports book manager came over and said, "Congratulations, Mr. Riccio. Looks like you had a nice hit today. You won $162,000!"

I was thrilled. It was sort of like winning the lottery again. Even so, I was annoyed it took them so long to tell me my results and wasn't about to keep that account open anymore. They had made me wait more than an hour just to hear how much I'd won. "I want my money now," I told him. "I'll bet with cash from now on."

I thought it would take a long time to count out all the cash I won, but they paid me in bricks of $50,000 each. There's $5,000 in each stack, and they rubber band 10 stacks together to make a brick. It took them less than 30 seconds to pay off the whole amount: $50,000, $100,000, $150,000 with the bricks, $155,000, $160,000 with the stacks, and a fast count of $100 bills to $162,000. "Thank you," the lady said as the window slammed back down. That was quick!

I went back up to my room and spread the cash all over the bed. My wife was there with our new baby. It was kind of surreal seeing my three-week-old baby in a pile of cash so large that most people don't see in their entire lives.

The next day I bet a few thousand dollars on the pro NFL games, which is something I know a lot about. I'm an expert on pro NFL games, but I lost every bet that Sunday. Some expert I am. Still, I was up way more than $150,000 for the trip, and Richie got the money he needed.

Nineteen eighty-nine was the best year of my life! I got married, won the lottery, had a daughter, broke a Vegas sports book, and business was booming. But as the law of gravity says, what goes up must come down.

Irene and I with our three-week-old daughter Angela in
October 1989 with $162,000 cash that I won in Vegas.

Chapter Eleven

LAS VEGAS
EARLY 90s

I was still on a winning streak. It seemed like everything I touched turned to gold. I continued dealing on the SportsNet. Most of my business involved pre-selling baseball cards to stores before they were even issued. The card shops were allocated one case of each new product from the factory and needed to buy from sources like me in order to have enough new inventories to stay in business. Everybody was trying to get product. It was never hard to sell product at that time—obtaining the stuff at good prices was the trick. That's why we all dealt in pre-sales.

I needed to get out there and find more cases to supply the demand for them. Big companies like Costco were allotted 40 or 50 cases, and I'd make deals with the managers by giving them $1,000 for the opportunity to buy some of their stock before it hit their sales floor. Then I would resell them for a 300 percent profit to other shops and even more to the retail customers in my store. We were buying cases for $600 and selling them for $1,800. People were literally waiting in line to buy the product. It was a crazy time in the business. Prices were shooting through the roof, but it couldn't last.

Before I knew it, I had $600,000 or $700,000 worth of inventory. In addition to my new house with its own strip-mall, I now had

May 25, 1991, Irene and I welcomed the birth of our second daughter, Clairissa Irene Riccio.

hundreds of thousands of dollars in the bank. I was worth well over a million dollars! Even better, Irene and I had our second daughter. Clairissa Irene Riccio was born on May 25, 1991. This time it was a natural childbirth, and the delivery went much more smoothly than the birth of our first child.

I probably went to Las Vegas for card conventions 5 or 6 times over the next year. Each time I made $20- to $30,000 in sales at the show, yet most of the time I came home broke. I gambled away everything I made. No big deal, I thought at the time, I was making more than that each week in my business. At least up until that point.

The whole business with pre-selling was risky. It was like playing stock market futures. Soon enough the card companies got smart and realized that people like me were buying their product, marking it up, and making triple what they sold it for. They decided to increase the cost of the cards and allow stores to buy more, so collectors wouldn't go to brokers like me to get the product. Instead of allocating one case to a store, they suddenly let each store have 10 to 20 cases. They also started printing cards around the clock. Supply was going up, while demand was going down.

So there I was, committed to buying hundreds of cases months in advance at as much as $1,000 a case. By the time the cards actually came out and arrived in my shop, they were worth less than half of what I'd paid for them. The whole business reversed. All of a sudden there were too many cards floating around. We were spending around $100,000 for about 100 cases of new product each month, but instead of our new monthly product being worth $200,000 like it would have been just a year before, it was now worth $50,000 at best. Instead of making $100,000 each month, we were now losing $50,000 each month. My business was taking a terrible hit. To make matters worse, I started taking gambling to another level in an effort to compensate for my business losses. It didn't work.

The first big bet I made was on the Super Bowl. I liked John Elway and took Denver plus 13 and a half points, but by the first quarter the score was 28-3, and the 49ers ended up blowing them out. I lost $50,000 on that game and immediately thought *I've got to get that money back*. I continued gambling more. Then my business continued to tank.

By the beginning of 1992, I was tapped out financially even though I still had a lot of inventory. The entire card business was shot. People were practically giving away collections they previously thought would pay to put their kids through college.

I committed to buying inventory from another wholesaler, and we contracted for a deal worth about $100,000. He gave me two-week terms to pay and delivered the product to me, but I lost about $50,000 by the time I sold it. I suddenly had to come up with the money to pay but had no extra cash. At the time we made the deal, the product had been worth what he charged. I thought it would go up in value like it had in past years, but this year it went down.

All the great luck I had from the last two years was gone. Now everything I touched was literally turning to shit. I sold some stuff and scraped about $65,000 together but was still $35,000 short. So I headed for Vegas to try to turn it into the $100,000 I owed. Once again my wife thought this was crazy, naturally. She said, "Give him the money you have, and tell him you'll give him the rest soon. He'll understand. He knows you lost money on this deal!"

"I don't want to do that." I was embarrassed and knew he wouldn't want to hear it. I envisioned him calling SportsNet and talking shit about my company. I didn't want any other dealers to know my company was hurting financially.

"Whatever you do, stop gambling!" My wife said. Of course I didn't listen. I know now that my problem with gambling stemmed from the fact that I had been lucky so many times in my past. Gambling seemed like a logical solution to my troubles. Whenever something went wrong, the first thing I thought was that my problems will disappear if I take the cash I have, parlay it, and win a ton of money. As crazy as it seems now, it actually worked several times when I badly needed it. So why wouldn't I go to the well once again?

I headed to Vegas with my $65,000 cashier's check, deposited it in the sports book cage account, placed a few baseball parlay bets, and then went up to my room. That's when I noticed that the girl at the sports book made a mistake on my tickets and put the Braves to win instead of

the under in one game. I ran back downstairs and got to the
window an hour before that game started, but the manager
wouldn't let me change the ticket because one of the other
games on the ticket had already started. I had real bad
feelings about everything at that point.

Of course the Atlanta Braves lost 3-2. The over/under
was 8, and the teams scored 5. Since all my other games were
winners, I would've won about $75,000 if that girl had gotten
my bet right. I was physically sick. At first I wanted to go
home and take it as a sign that I should never gamble again,
but then I got mad and went down to complain to the manager.

"I know what happened really stinks, Tom," the
sports book manager said, "but there are gaming laws, and
we just can't change a parlay ticket after one of the games
starts. You have plenty left on your account. Give it
another shot."

I should've left right then and sued them later, but
instead I kept trying. I wanted to win more than ever, but I
didn't come close and lost all my money.

I went home but was so upset that I couldn't think of
anything else. I tried to stop the check by calling the bank,
but they told me I couldn't stop the cashier's check unless it
was recovered by me. I called the sports manager again and
asked him to pay me for their mistake. He said he was going
away for the weekend, but the check wouldn't leave the
casino cage until Monday morning. He suggested that I come
back and try to win the check back. This guy's employee cost
me $75,000, and his only answer was to throw more money
at him. Now I was extremely pissed!

I got an idea and went back to my bank, bought a $65
cashier's check, and flew back out to Vegas. I marched right
up to the casino cage and asked to see my $65,000 cashier's
check that was on deposit. To my amazement, the lady pulled
out the check and showed it to me. I took the $65,000 check,
turned my back to the cage, pulled out the $65 check, ripped
it up, and left the pieces on the counter. The lady thought I
ripped up the $65,000 check, but that check was in my
pocket. I told her why I ripped up the check, and she called
the manager and security. I didn't think they'd let me go, but
the manager asked me to leave the ripped check pieces on the

counter, go get some sleep, and we'd figure it out in the morning. I just left the casino and went home with my $65,000 check. My rage turned to relief.

By the time I made it back to my house, there were 10 phone messages from the casino. The phone rang again and it was them. "That was a real nice scam Mr. Riccio, but we want our check back."

I responded, "Your check? Look, you know exactly what happened. I was screwed by your employee for more than $75,000. I figure you guys still owe me $10,000. Where's the rest of my money?"

The head of security started yelling. "If this was 20 years ago, they'd find you face down in the desert!"

"Shut up, Angelo!" the casino manager then said to me, "He doesn't mean that."

"Here is what I'll do," I proposed, "The check is deposited back into my account. Let's both tell the truth about what happened and let an arbitrator decide who gets the money."

They tried to negotiate with me, but I strongly felt they were wrong and wanted someone else to confirm it. Soon it was clear to everyone that there had been no theft. The check was made out to me, and the casino teller handed it back to me. The only issue was if the casino was liable for their error that cost me $75,000. They finally agreed to arbitration, and to my surprise, at the hearing they told the truth about their screw-up that cost me the money. They also said they had no means to correct the error.

The arbitrator ruled in my favor, and I got my $65,000 back. This time, I took my wife's advice and gave the money to the broker I owed $100,000 and explained that I didn't have the other $35,000. The broker said, "Tom, we've been doing business for a while. We're in the same business; I know you lost money on our deal. You're a good guy, pay me the rest when you can."

The next week a new product came out—a basketball series featuring a rookie card for Shaquille O'Neal that rejuvenated the whole card business. Everybody went crazy for Shaq. Cases I had bought for $700 or $800 were suddenly worth $2,000. Within a couple of weeks, I made a bunch of money and was able to pay the broker back in full.

Shaquille O'Neal and his rookie card saved everybody in the card business for a while, but by 1994, all the dealers were losing again. The card business went downhill for good. The whole industry was on life support. And so was I.

Chapter Twelve

BUSTED AGAIN
1994

I was sitting in my hot tub one day and grabbed the remote to turn on the TV. As I was flipping though the channels, I saw the closed-circuit feed to my shop out front. I had a girl working there and watched as she handed some kid an expensive baseball card set. The kid pulled out a price guide while he was flipping though the set, looking nervously back at the girl who wasn't paying much attention. I jumped out of the tub and ran up to my shop just as the punk was leaving. I grabbed his price guide, and sure enough there was about $1,000 worth of cards, including vintage Mantle and Aaron cards, that he had slipped into the book while looking through the card set.

I was a kid once and knew what happens when you call the cops. The parents are put through hell, they waste the victim's time in court, the kids get a record, and the courts make money from the fines they impose. How the hell does that help me? I developed my own law when it came to catching punks ripping me off: Once I catch them, I find them guilty, and then I fine them double the price of the items they tried to steal from me. I don't want to call the police on kids, but I want them to pay. I give them the option of paying the fine I impose or letting a real judge decide after the police are called. They always pick my fine. In this particular case, I got this kid's name, phone number, and bike. I gave him half an hour to come back to my shop with his card collection. When he returned I picked out about $2,000 worth of cards from his collection to take care of his fine.

One time I caught a kid stealing from me at a card show. I grabbed his backpack, and sure enough there was my stolen card, along with about $3,000 worth of other cards. I took all his cards and kicked him out of the show. Most of what was in his backpack had just been stolen by him at the show, and I returned them all to the dealers whose stickers were on the cards. Most of the other dealers wanted me to call the police on these kid crooks, but I never thought that was the fairest way to resolve it—not for the kids or me. Every kid I caught agreed to my terms and paid me their fine. I wish I'd had the same opportunity to take care of a situation like that when I was a kid.

Thieving kids were always a nuisance, but I had bigger problems. Cards were dead. My business was dying, and I knew I had to diversify. A pawn shop was up the road from my shop, and people started bringing in all kinds of stuff to try to sell me. I had people coming in with coins, jewelry, chains, and other stuff like that. Soon enough my card business became almost like another pawn shop. I was buying stuff really cheap and reselling it to the pawn shop up the street. I also used the local pawn shop to verify that the gold and jewels people were trying to unload were real. That business was going fine and kept me afloat for a while.

A guy I had never seen before came in one day trying to sell two cases of 1989 Upper Deck cards, which ran about $2,000 per case. He also had a box of foreign gold coins and a huge box full of foreign silver and copper coins. I had no idea if they were real or even what country they were from. I didn't deal much in coins, mostly because of the incident I had with them in the past.

These coins appeared to be genuine, but for all I knew, they were fakes. "They're from Colombia. This is a Colombian king on the coins. They're all solid gold," the guy assured me. I wasn't so sure. "Come on, 20 grand for the whole lot," he asked.

"Nah, I just want the cards," I told him and ended up doing a $3,000 deal with him for the two cases of cards and box of gold coins. As it turned out, all the gold was real, and I made about $50,000 flipping the gold coins to other shops.

The guy with the coins came in again a couple of weeks later and said, "Hey, do you want the rest of the stuff? I told you they were all real. I shouldn't have given you such a good deal but I needed the money."

I didn't think the other coins had as much value, but I wound up giving him $1,500 for the copper and silver coins. One of the guys I had been selling the silver and copper coins to had a shop in Glendale. I traded him some of these coins for gold pieces. A couple of months later, he called and asked if I had any coins left. "Just the copper crap, all of the gold and silver is gone," I told him.

"Well, come by my shop. I think I have a buyer."

"Why don't you bring him here?"

"No, come on, this buyer's got a ton of money. He's looking to buy a lot of stuff. Bring the coins over here."

I went over there to meet the buyer, and he examined a few of the coins I had brought with me. The majority was still at home in my safe. "How ya doing? These are your coins?"

"Yeah, they're mine." I said.

"FBI. You're under arrest for trading in stolen goods." Turned out the guy who'd sold me the coins had been all over the L.A. area trying to sell this collection, and people knew who he was. The agents interviewed my two employees who were working when I bought the collection. Apparently this was a collection worth several hundred thousand dollars, and I paid less than one percent of what it was actually worth.

"It's common knowledge that this was a stolen collection," the FBI guy said. That was news to me, and after checking out my story with my employees and other dealers, they let me go. I gave them the rest of the coins and hired a lawyer, but the FBI was done with me.

Next thing I knew the Buena Park police showed up to arrest me for receiving stolen goods in their area. "You admitted that you bought this collection in our town; we're getting calls from Long Beach where they were stolen. We have to arrest you." We did the same whole song and dance again. They were trying very hard to get me to tell them some names and agree to testify against people I didn't even know, but I had no idea how that guy got the collection he sold me and would not agree to testify against people I'd never even heard of before.

A few weeks later the Long Beach police came knocking on my door and arrested me. This time they were insistent I knew the actual thieves and claimed I had some inside knowledge because of my record as a teenager. These cops wanted to bust me. It was a similar situation to when I was a kid, but that time I knew the collection was stolen because I was there when we walked off with them. This time I had no idea where the coins came from or that this collection had been stolen. I got out on a $20,000 bond and went to court.

While I was out on bail, I moved out of my home to put the complex up for sale because the card business was now non-existent. My complex was worth about $400,000, and I probably owned half of that in equity. Two weeks after we moved out, I got a call from the tenants who were still in my store units, saying there was some sort of problem. Homeless people were camped out in the house that I had recently vacated. They punched holes in the ceiling, tore the cabinet doors off, broke the heating, destroyed the air conditioning, and totally ruined the place. They were on a rampage. Whenever my tenants went over to confront the homeless gang, they ran away.

I went over to inspect and saw my place, which was trashed. The squatters had left a bunch of clothes and junk on the porch, and I was so mad when I saw it that I built up a huge pile, poured some butane on it, and set it on fire. Every last bit of what they'd left on my property went up in flames. I did this right in front of my tenants. I was so upset at their vandalism that I just reacted without thinking. Literally the second that I tossed the wooden match I thought, *What the hell am I doing?* All I can compare it to is when people pull the trigger of a gun and wish they could take it back. I understand that feeling because I'll always regret that incident. I only hurt myself.

I got put back in jail. The Long Beach police interviewed my employees again and continued their investigation. They kept hammering at me, bringing up the old charge. "You are a career criminal; as a teenager you were dealing in stolen goods…a $500,000 collection and none of it was recovered…and the arson…reckless endangerment….” I was offered a deal for time served if I admitted I knew I had bought stolen goods.

My lawyer advised me. “If you take this deal, your business will be ruined, basically.”

I didn't care about my business, but no one had told me the stuff was stolen.

“I don't know how they can prove you knew it was stolen; we have your employees' statement,” said my lawyer. I decided to go for it and have a trial. My other choice was to admit to the judge that I knew I was dealing in stolen goods, and I would have gotten off with time served and restitution, but I couldn't do it. I wouldn't do it.

The prosecution kept trying to make deals with me, coming to me trying to get me to name the guys who actually stole the stuff, but I had no idea, or I certainly would have told them. I knew nothing more than what I'd told the police—I'd never seen that guy before and had no idea the stuff was stolen. I had been dealing those coins for more than a year before I was even arrested! Nobody had said a thing!

My trial lasted for three days. Then the jurors took a vote each day. I later learned that on the first day, nine jurors thought I was innocent, and three thought I was guilty. Then they asked the judge for instructions. “What if Mr. Riccio didn't know the goods were stolen when he bought them, but after he sold a bunch of them off, several months later, he figured it out?”

“If at any point up to one second before he was arrested he thought the coins were stolen, he's guilty of receiving stolen goods,” the judge told them sternly.

The jury returned to the judge at the end of the second day and told him that they were deadlocked. It was a hung jury. Several jurors had switched their votes to guilty, but there were still some holdouts. The judge said, “You're making great progress. I don't care if it takes you another eight weeks, we'll come back every day until you do your civic duty.” This worried the jurors. One was a student and had exams coming up. Nobody else on the jury wanted to miss that much work.

"You have an hour and a half left today," said the judge. "Go back in there, I'm not releasing anyone."

They came back 45 minutes later and found me guilty. It was up to the judge to sentence me. "The business of dealing in stolen goods is a despicable one. It's people like you who promote the drug problems in this country today," the judge said. "There are heroin addicts because of your business and the way you conduct it. People steal to feed their drug habits because they know they have you to go to. Many lives are going down the tubes because of people like you and your business."

I had to interrupt, "What are you talking about? I don't even know a heroin addict!"

"Shut up!" the judge said. "Be quiet while I'm speaking. I'm sentencing you to the maximum: five years. You've done this before; maybe you'll learn your lesson this time."

That day in court was the saddest day of my life. The day they sentenced me happened to be my daughter Angela's fifth birthday. She asked me, "Daddy, when are you coming home?" The judge had just sentenced me to five years in state prison. I hadn't laid eyes on my wife or kids for months while I was in jail, but Irene started in with, "What's this about the judge saying you're dealing with heroin addicts now?" I was too depressed to explain.

A few weeks later and feeling totally defeated, I pled No Contest to the arson charge for lighting the homeless vandals' junk on fire at my house. The important thing was that I got no extra time for burning the crap, but I did get the five years for dealing in stolen goods. It was devastating, but I didn't want to fight it. I just wanted to get everything behind me, but I really hate the arson charge on my record. Again, I am not justifying any of the things I've done, but I lit that junk on fire on my own property. Even though I didn't serve any time for it, it looks like the worst thing I ever did in my life.

To add insult to injury, one of the homeless people who destroyed my place actually filed a claim against me for burning their crap. While I was sitting in the holding cell handcuffed, my lawyer stopped by and said, "I've got the title to your truck here; you need to sign it over to me for legal bills." It was my very last piece of property; the last thing I owned. There was nothing I could do but sign it over.

I make hundreds of deals each year, and it's impossible to know if any one collection is stolen or not. I realized that even though no one told me that stuff was stolen, lots of signs made it very obvious that it was. There were several other dealers who dealt with coins from that same stolen collection, and none of them got arrested or charged except me. My past mistakes should have taught me not to have taken any chances at that stage of my life, but I did and can't complain about what happened to me. As I sat there feeling very depressed, I looked back and knew that I had only myself to blame. Who should feel sorry for me? I've been blessed, over and over in my life, but once again, I pissed it all away.

Chapter Thirteen

SOLEDAD STATE PRISON
1994 -1997

My brother sent my wife a couple thousand dollars so she and my daughters could come visit me in Soledad State Prison. Even though I had no violence on my record, the escape from federal prison got me placed in this Mid-Level security facility. It would take some time to arrange the visiting day, but at least I knew I would be seeing her and the kids soon.

Boy, do you learn a lot about the state of race relationships in America when you go to prison. In federal prison it isn't as bad, but in state prison it's unbelievable. The first thing the convicts tell you when you get inside is you're not allowed to speak or deal with anybody outside your own race without permission from one of the leaders of your race. That was a bit of a problem for me. Pieces of crap and great people exist in every race; I wanted to mix with whomever I wanted.

The Mexicans are even stranger, because if you're a Mexican from Southern California you're not allowed to socialize with Mexicans from Northern California. Two men might literally be blood brothers, but if one lives in Oakland and one lives in L.A. and they wind up in the same prison, they have to fight each other to the death over their gang affiliations. There are some minor differences in policies between the two: Northern California Mexicans can hang out with the blacks, but the Southern California Mexicans can't.

When you get to prison, you're classified as Black, White, Mexican, Hispanic, or Other. When I first arrived in Soledad, the whites—or "Woods" as they call themselves—

were very nice to me. "Hey, you need some toothpaste?" Things like that. Then they started telling me the rules and things went downhill.

If the leaders from the Woods asked you to go to the yard for a possible conflict with another race, you are supposed to just show up to risk your life in a possible race war without asking any questions. I'd always ask what the problem was, and most of the time they wouldn't answer. That usually means it's a drug deal gone bad, or the other very big issue in prison—disrespect. A lot of violent fights occur in prison, and it's almost always about someone disrespecting another inmate. I don't understand it. Although some decent people are incarcerated, most of the inmates are there for good reasons. They're pieces of shit that need to be there! Why should I care if they disrespect me? As long as they don't put their hands on me, I'm fine with the disrespect. Call me anything you want. I won't lose any sleep at night. It would hurt me much more if someone I respected or cared about disrespected me. Frankly, I don't give a shit!

Everyone in prison must work or get locked up in the hole. At first I was assigned to work in the Prison Chapel where I cleaned up the chapel after every service. The Prison Chapel is a very interesting study in religion. Many different religions congregate in the chapel. Nearly every hour there's a different religion gathering for a service, and they all seem to have one thing in common. If you are Catholic, Jewish, Baptist, Buddhist, Muslim, or any of the other dozens of popular religions, you could commit any sin in the book but are forgiven if you are a member of their group; however, if you are not a member of their religion, you're doomed to hell.

*   *   *

I started up a trading business and was willing to deal with anybody of any color as long as they had something legal to trade (I never dealt with drugs or contraband). It wasn't even about money; my brothers would have happily lent me any money I needed. I wasn't dependent on making a few dollars a day in prison, but I loved to wheel and deal and that made the time pass by. I simply could not sit still and do nothing. Like a compulsion, I couldn't stop dealing. Buying, selling, trading, repairing.... I enjoyed all that.

I bought a broken Walkman radio from an inmate cheap because the headphones had a short in the wire and didn't work. I fixed the short, the radio worked, and I traded it for a stack of smut magazines. When they stopped allowing naked girl magazines in the prison, the value went up for the ones that were already in there. A guy named Flaco made custom cigarette lighter holders out of popsicle sticks and needed small photos of nude girls for his holders. The back of my magazines featured dozens of ads with the small nude photos he needed, and I worked on taking out the photos to sell to Flaco for 25¢ each. I had the pictures piled all over my desk in the Prison Chapel when a chaplain walked in. He wasn't happy!

"Do you really think this kind of material is appropriate here in God's house?" Chaplain Bob asked as he fired me and sent me back to my prison dorm. I knew selling smut out of the chapel was wrong, but I never thought that "God's House" was located in the Soledad State Prison. I hope they parole him soon.

Next they assigned me to pick up trash out on the prison yard. I'm one of the best workers in the world when I'm working for myself; otherwise, I'm not worth a shit. As an employee in prison picking up cigarette butts in the yard, I wasn't even worth the 11¢ an hour that they were paying me. Prison Guard Owens wasn't a bad guy, and he'd explain to me that he'd get in trouble from his supervisor if the yard was a mess. I made a deal with him to make sure my yard was spotless, as long as he didn't care how it got done. I had three or four inmates who were begging to do my work on the yard in exchange for a few cigarettes or a shot of coffee: My yard was by far the cleanest. I got my sleep, and my work got done—I just wasn't gonna be the guy to do it.

I tried to make the best of my shitty situation and was determined to keep busy. I started up lots of small businesses in prison right away. I fixed radios, oiled old fans, and repaired headphones. I bought and sold cigarettes, candy, coffee, and food. All the other inmates called me "Trader." I always loved trading—baseball cards as a kid or cigarettes in prison—and I couldn't stop making deals. I just needed to occupy my time and mind, but as usual my luck didn't hold.

Prisoners are very respectful of inmates who've been convicted of robbery, drugs, rape, and murder. Believe it or not, the more violet the crime, the more respected you are, but two things they don't accept is a child molester or a rat (snitch). The most common thing inmates do when they don't like a fellow convict is falsely label them. Usually they start a rumor that the convict is a rat because it's pretty easy to prove with your arrest report that you're not a molester, but it's hard to prove you're not a rat.

It happens almost every day in prison, and it's truly amazing how easy it is for some asshole coward who's afraid to confront an inmate they don't like to just put a "Rat Jacket" on a guy and then sit back and watch all the other morons play right into it. After this one little Mexican punk bugged me for the hundredth time for a candy bar, I told him to stay the fuck away from me and he said, "It's like that, huh?"

I told him, "It's EXACTLY like that!!"

Then he said, "Okay man, you fuck with one little bean, you're fucking with the whole burrito!" which means he's gonna sic his gang on me.

The next thing I knew all these Mexicans were coming up to me asking, "Hey Trader, why is everyone saying you're a rat?"

It's real simple to use common sense and break it down for them. "Why am I a rat?" I asked. "Name one incident where anyone ever got in trouble because of me." Of course they couldn't, but that didn't matter.

One day I was out playing Frisbee in the yard when a couple of Mexican guys approached me, asking me to fix some headphones. I was headed back inside to shower and told them I'd speak to them later, but one of them kept calling me over. "Trader, come over here, I want to show you something." I could tell he and his friends were trying to keep me away from my bunk area; I looked over at my locker and saw some other guys bending the metal locker door back with a mop handle and grabbing my stuff inside.

"Hey, what's up?" I shouted.

Five or six little bald-headed punks immediately surrounded me, kicking and beating and punching me. One guy hit me with the mop handle. A few inmates just stood around and watched; they did nothing to help me out. One little guy was coming at me from the side, and I cracked his head against the wall. It left a bloodstain. The guards finally came, and all the Mexicans said I jumped their little homie with the bloody head. I was handcuffed and put in the hole. My ribs were cracked, and I had lots of cuts and bruises from the gang of punks attacking me, but I was the one that got charged with assault.

"Yeah, you're going to get five more years added onto your sentence for assault!" the guard taunted.

The next day I sat in a jail cell beat up but still feeling okay, because I knew that after a year of not seeing them, my wife and kids were coming to visit. Then a counselor came over and said, "I've got a letter and documents for you from your wife."

I opened it up and saw divorce documents with a note from Irene that read, "This marriage is a joke and I'm divorcing you."

This was definitely the worst day of my life. I had broken ribs, was beat all to hell, facing an additional five years on top of my sentence, and not only was my wife not going to visit me, she was also divorcing me. I'd never known why people give up in life and just jump off a bridge until that day. I'm glad no high bridges were in the hole. I sank into a deep depression and slept all the time. I even refused to wake up for meals.

My mother had sent me a subscription to *USA Today* so I would have something to occupy my mind while I was in solitary confinement, but I couldn't even read it. I couldn't concentrate on anything. I just slept 20 hours a day.

The prison kangaroo court held a hearing where they told me, "So Mr. Riccio, you want us to believe that all those guys are lying, and you are the innocent one?"

"Yes sir," I continued, "I know it must be hard for you to believe that there are some bad guys here in your prison, but I just ran into about a half dozen of them who jumped me when I caught them breaking into my locker. Check my record, I've never been in a fight outside of prison in my entire life. If you check their records, I bet anything you can figure out exactly who the violent ones are." They decided to keep me in solitary while they conducted a further investigation of the incident.

Fortunately, some of the inmate "snitches" finally told the officials what actually happened the day I was jumped, and they dropped the assault charges against me. I got transferred to Avenol State Prison and wound up doing the rest of my time with no further incident.

Chapter Fourteen

LONG BEACH
1997

I got out of prison in October 1997. My wife had officially divorced me, and it was clear my in-laws had pressured her into it. For the life of me, I could never understand why they disliked me so much. I realize I had my share of problems and wasn't sure how I'd respond if my daughter brought home an ex-con to marry, but at that point I had known my in-laws for several years and tried to do everything I could to be a good son-in-law.

When I was riding pretty high and had lots of money, I was happy to help my in-laws by fixing up things at their house, buying them a car when they needed one, and giving them money on several occasions, but as soon as I got locked up for buying that collection, they had Irene's phone blocked. I couldn't call collect even though I had my brother send money for the phone bill. It was hard not being able to speak to my young daughters for years. Now that I was free, they did everything to try and prevent me from getting back together with Irene. The only reason I could think of was Irene was a good daughter (their slave girl who drove them around and did everything for them), and they didn't want to lose her back to me.

I was supposed to check in with my parole officer in Long Beach on Monday but it was Friday, and the very first thing I did was make a deal with the cabbie to take me straight down to Oceanside, near San Diego, where my now ex-wife was living with my in-laws and our daughters. Irene started right in, "My father says that we shouldn't be together. I can't go back with you. This is twice in your life you've been locked up. I can't trust that this won't happen again."

"I'm out now," I told her, "and it is not gonna happen again. Let's give us another shot." My wife wouldn't budge; she didn't want to get back together, but we did get to spend a great weekend together in my hotel room with our daughters.

My brother lent me a few thousand dollars, and I saw an ad in the local newspaper for a 1985 Chrysler New Yorker for $1,000. I just needed a car, any car, and I had no way to run around shopping for one. So I talked the seller into showing up at my hotel with the big old gas guzzler, got him down to $700, and paid all of it in cash. Then I drove back up to Long Beach to check in with my parole officer.

My brother-in-law called my parole officer to report that I had come down to San Diego and contacted my ex-wife, which was in direct violation of my parole terms. There's a general belief among those who've done time that you never want to be assigned to a female parole officer. Supposedly they'll throw you back in prison at the drop of a hat because they love to exert their power. However, my female parole officer was very fair.

"There's only one thing I don't like Mr. Riccio." She continued, "People who lie. If you lie to me, I'm going to lock you back up. So no matter how bad it is, tell the truth. Now I'm going to ask you once: Did you go down to Oceanside without permission to see your wife and kids?"

"Okay, I'm not gonna lie to you. I hadn't seen my wife and kids in years, and I had to see them. I'm sorry."

"If you need to go down there, tell me and I'll give you a pass, but make sure you get permission and stay away from your in-laws. I can tell they're assholes who are trying to use me to put you back in prison." We got along great after that.

I was surprised that people I have done business with before I was locked up didn't want anything more to do with me. People who were acting like they were my friends and asking for big credit lines when things were going great now couldn't find time to speak with me to see if I could help them sell their inventory. However, I heard that one guy wanted to see me.

Lowell was a weekend card dealer, a real character who was always doing something with his hot Filipino girlfriend Gigi. Lowell always invited me to join them. He would say, "Hey Mötley Crüe's in town, let's all go hang out with them!" Turned out he actually knew them. When Mötley Crüe was just starting out, he was their photographer and was credited with the photos on their first album cover. I would've loved to go but always seemed to have a pregnant wife at the time. Even though I said no, he kept asking me to hang out.

Years ago before I was arrested, Lowell showed up at my shop with hundreds of hockey cards. "Hey, look at these Wayne Gretzky Rookie cards. They're all counterfeit! I caught these kids at a friend's shop trying to sell these fake cards! I did what you do at the shows—confiscated everything! I gave him a choice: I'd take them or we could call the police. So they let me have them, and I took them off the market. What should I do with these phony cards?" Lowell was a real hockey nut; he knew his cards. They looked like the real deal, but they had smooth edges whereas the real cards were rough-edged. That was the only way to tell. Those Gretzky cards were easily worth $600 bucks apiece if they had been real. Lowell wasn't dishonest and wasn't going to try to pass them off as real. We stamped them all "COUNTERFEIT" and sold them at shows for $10 each. He easily could have fooled a lot people and made a ton of money, but he didn't. I respected him for that.

Lowell and I had one thing in common. We always seemed to have some get-rich-quick scheme, but more often than not, it got us in trouble. When Lowell's name came up a couple of times, and someone gave me a note with his phone number asking about me to call him, I hesitated but didn't have many options. So I called him and set up a meeting. Lowell treated me like a long-lost brother; he was the only person who was happy to see me again.

We went back to Lowell's home office where he told me all about this new website called eBay. It was 1997, and no one knew about eBay, but Lowell was one of the first people to use it. Baseball card shops were dying, and he would ask people who were closing their shops if he could put their inventory on eBay. It was very successful. He taught me all the ins and outs of eBay and gave me some work helping him sell his stuff while I learned about the new Internet business.

I'll always remember how I was looking for help from others to return the many favors I'd done for them in the past, but it was Lowell who found me and went out of his way to help me out. Lowell is a bit of a crazy pain in the ass from time to time, but there will always be a place in my heart for his help in getting me back on my feet and being a real friend when I was fresh out of prison. One day at work Lowell said, "Hey Tom, you know my wife Gigi has like 27 sisters."

"Yeah, so?"

"Well, I know you just got divorced. Why don't you marry one of her sisters so they could come here from the Philippines? They'll pay you $10,000."

Wow! I needed $10,000, but I didn't want to marry anyone at that point. I was concentrating on getting my life back together; I wasn't going to get married even though I badly needed the money.

One day we got paid on a deal, and Lowell had an idea: "Hey, come on Tom, let's go to the casino. Some Australian ponies are racing today!"

I knew absolutely nothing about horses, but we went anyway. I gave him the $100 I just got paid to bet for me. I started watching the races and noticed that the odds the track posted were exactly right on almost every race. The horse favored 1-1 came in first. The horse at 2-1 came in second. The horse at 3-1 odds always came in third and so on. Very few of the long shots ever came in. The whole thing seemed pretty simple to me, and about halfway through the races, I finally said, "Lowell, why not bet on the first, second and third horse? They always come in that way!"

"No, no, you can't make any money that way. I'm going for the long shots."

"But they're not coming in, Lowell! Why not bet on the favorites?"

Lowell's system wasn't working, and we were losing our shirts. Then I discovered trifectas. If we were to bet on the first three horses to cross the finish line in first, second, and third place, and the horses finished in that exact order, we would win a lot of cash. Then a man approached us. "I've got a double race trifecta ticket here, and I've already won the first one. I've got to leave now, so I'll sell you this ticket for 50 bucks. You choose the second trifecta. You could win the jackpot."

I studied the ticket. The man paid only two dollars for the ticket, but he had already won the first trifecta with a couple of long shots, which was hard to believe because it was the ONLY race where a long shot came in. All we had to do was pick the first, second, and third horse on the second race. We could bet the favorites and win big. "Hey Lowell, give me fifty bucks. I'm gonna bet on the favorites for this ticket. We could win big!"

"Tom, we're here to bet the Australian races not that shit. Let's stick to the plan."

"Give me my 50 bucks Lowell. I've got a good feeling." Opportunity seemed to be knocking, and I wanted to let it in.

"You don't have 50 bucks left." The two of us argued back and forth and finally the guy got sick of us and left. Naturally the three horses I would have picked—the clear-cut odds on favorites for first, second and third places— won the race. I would have won $21,000. I knew nothing about racing but had that vibe and just couldn't get Lowell to go along with it. I was pissed. "Lowell, look at that, I could have won that jackpot!" I really needed that money. The angel of mercy had knocked on my door again, but this time Lowell slammed it.

I ended up losing more than I had and owed Lowell $100. On the way out, Lowell said he had to get his kid a toy. Before he went to the gift shop, he handed me $100 and asked me to pay the slots for him until he got back. I placed the money in the slot machine and 10 minutes later the bells rung crazy. I won $5,000 for Lowell. He took the $5,000, thanked me, and squashed the $100 I owed him from losing on his races.

Another time Lowell and I took a business trip to San Francisco to sell some comic art to a millionaire college kid. This kid's father had just bought the Duracell battery company when it was losing money. He fired 75 percent of the employees, and when the company showed a profit for the next quarter, he sold it for millions in profit. The dad gave his 19-year-old son a million dollars to invest anyway he wanted, and the son went on eBay to start buying. That's where we met him, and we had a great time helping him spend his cash on our shit.

After we did our deal with the Duracell heir, we made more money than we hoped for, and we felt like celebrating. Lowell knew of every weird place in every city, so I let him drag me along to some place he'd read about on the Internet. I had no idea what I was getting into.

The place looked like an old creepy looking castle. We each paid a $15 entrance fee and wandered through the huge house with other customers who ranged from business attired men and women to transsexual ghouls. The place was very dark, and it was the kind of place that you really wanted some light—just to make sure there wasn't anyone standing too close to you.

There were about 100 rooms in the mansion, and they were rooms full of masked leather-clad people with whips, regular couples having sex, and dominatrix tying business-men up and whipping them. Apparently any of the customers could just go into a room to do strange things with each other while others watched. The best way to describe it was like the weirdest Triple X Halloween Haunted House you could ever imagine. Lowell loved it. "Is this genius or what? There should be one of these in every city! Maybe we should open a few of these down in Los Angeles. What do you think Tom?"

"That was very interesting, Lowell. I'm glad I can say that I've seen something like that in my life, but lets get the hell out of here!"

"No way, I want to go through it again!" That was Lowell.

*   *   *

I was starting to figure out my new life as a free guy just out of prison, and one of my parole conditions was to see a state psychiatrist who asked me, "What are your plans for the future? Where do you see yourself in one year?"

"Most importantly, I'd like to have my wife and kids back," I told him.

"What are the chances of that happening? How is that relationship?" he asked.

"Well, she divorced me and refuses to have anything to do with me. But I plan to have my family back within one year, and I'd like to be working in collectibles. I'm good in that business, and I'm using a new Internet site called eBay which is going pretty good. I'd also like to buy a house."

"Where are you living now?" the psychiatrist asked.

"I'm renting a room from an old lady," I said. "But within a year, I plan to have my own house, and I expect to pay off my debt of about 20 grand to my brothers and have about a $100,000 in the bank."

"So, to get this straight," the psych said, "you are renting a room. Your wife has no interest in getting back with you. You have no steady job and no money saved, but your one-year goal is to buy a house, get your wife and kids to come back and live with you, run your own business, pay off your debts, and have $100,000 in the bank. Is that right?"

"That's right," I said, happy with my plan.

"Mr. Riccio, let me make this very clear," the psychiatrist began, "you have delusions of grandeur. You are borderline bipolar and you need medication or you are doomed to fail. You need to get a regular job; I don't care if it's at McDonalds or digging ditches, but you cannot live with these delusional expectations, because when you fail to reach these unrealistic goals, it's inevitable that you will wind up right back in prison."

Wow! That guy wasn't much for building a guy's confidence, so screw him!

Chapter Fifteen

I LOVE LUCY
1998

I was renting a room in a 90-year-old lady's house. Thelma was surprisingly cool when my parole agent showed up. She didn't get spooked by the fact that I was on parole. I liked Thelma, but she was becoming dependant on me, and I never signed up to be there 24 hours a day. I only agreed to pay her for the room; however, I called social security and arranged for her to get more assistants to help her.

I tried over and over to get back with Irene but nothing worked. Whenever I went over to see my daughters, I took the kids a bunch of gifts, and my in-laws yelled at me for spending money on toys instead of giving more money to Irene. I wanted to try some way to make up for the time I'd missed being away from them, but I couldn't win.

With the few extra bucks I had, I bought my own computer on a site called Recycler.com to continue working on eBay and making deals.

I had a business trip to Vegas coming up, and out of the blue, my ex-wife called and said, "I'll come with you!" I was shocked, but okay. She came with me to Las Vegas and decided she wanted to get back together. "Just get us a place to stay, I'll come as soon as you arrange that," she told me.

*   *   *

I was still living at Thelma's house, but she was starting to slide. It got to where she'd get very upset with me if I stayed out all night. "Where have you been? I was waiting for my dinner!" she'd scold.

Thelma caught pneumonia that winter and collapsed in the hallway one night. She appeared to be getting better in the hospital for a while, and she even called me on the telephone ordering me to bring her a cheese sandwich. I was just making it when the hospital called back within 20 minutes to tell me she had passed away. That was a shock! Her son later called me and said, "Tom, we really appreciate all you did and you've been great, but we're selling the house to some fast escrow brokers, so you need to be out within two weeks."

I found another woman with a room to rent in her house, but this situation sucked. Whenever I wasn't at work, I was busy looking on the computer for a house to buy. The woman I was renting from was very lonely. Every night she used to come into my room and tell me her whole life story: the son who was on drugs, the boyfriend who'd left her.... I listened to it all even though I really just wanted to get some sleep.

One day my parole agent showed up to check on me, and an hour later I got a call from this woman's ex-boyfriend. "I think it's really shitty that you just get out of prison and move in with a nice lady without even telling her that you're an ex-con on parole! You need to get out as soon as possible. She wants you out!"

"I'm on parole for stolen property. It's not like I committed murder or anything," I protested.

"You've been in prison. She's afraid of you, so you need to get out now," he said. All I could say was I was sorry and planned to get out as fast as I could. I immediately doubled my efforts to find a house. I had a lot of obstacles to overcome looking for a place for my family. I couldn't even open a bank account. When I filed for bankruptcy in prison, my lawyers took everything. My officially divorced wife couldn't even open a bank account!

All I could qualify for were "owner will carry" properties. That's where the owner carries the mortgage, and it usually attracts people who can't get loans. Most of those places were in pretty dangerous locations: Lynwood, Compton, and other poor parts of Los Angeles. All the places I checked out were run down and in terrible neighborhoods.

I finally found a cute, little, green two-bedroom house in North Long Beach that shared a front lawn with a nice little old lady in a great multicultural neighborhood, but I needed to close the deal.

A friend of mine had told me years before not to use your own real estate agent if you want to buy a house. Hire the same agent who's selling the house to work for you, because this agent will receive both the buyer's and the seller's commission and will do whatever it takes to get you into that house. I called the agent on the sign in front of the house and said, "I want to buy this house."

"Who's your agent?" he asked.

"Here's what I'd like to do, hire you as my agent." California has plenty of laws in place to protect the buyer. If you're a decent negotiator, you can use their agent, and he'll help you get the house. The house was listed for $99,000. I wasn't about to let it go.

My new agent asked me, "What kind of offer do you want to put in?"

"Well, what's the lowest they'll accept?" I countered.

"It's pretty cheap right now, and it's an owner-will-carry property. They bought it for $139,000, so they're losing money already. Why don't you offer them $95,000?"

I put in the offer, and they came back with $97,000.

I had just over $5,000 in cash. The guy wanted $5,000 down and was willing to carry the loan. Most owners in this situation don't really care if you don't pay because they get a big deposit and put in a clause stating they get the house back and keep the deposit if you miss more than one payment. It's a very strict foreclosure law where the owner basically serves as the bank.

It was a few points higher than a bank at nine percent, but this was the best option available to me. I could always refinance the loan after I built my credit back up. I told the guy I'd take it as long as there were no closing costs because I didn't have a spare dime. We badly wanted this house; it was a decent little place in a decent neighborhood.

The agent called me right back and announced, "Done deal!"

I was very happy, but at the closing the owners said, "Okay, all we need is the $1,000 to cover taxes, and we're done."

"Wait a minute, I told you I have $5,000 and that's it. We had an agreement."

"It's in the closing agreement. You have to pay taxes," he sputtered.

"Absolutely not! You agreed to $5,000 out of my pocket, and that's all I have." The agent came back and said, "The house is in perfect condition. It's been inspected, no termites. So if you will waive the required termite tenting, I'll waive the taxes we prepaid." We wound up getting the cute, little, green house, and I knew it would be a great place to live for the foreseeable future. It cost me every cent I had, but I felt happy and extremely lucky.

*   *   *

A lot of people have told me, "Tom, you're such a good salesman. You could sell ice to an Eskimo!" But that's just not true. I'm a great sales guy only when I really like and believe in the item I'm selling. If I think something is a piece of shit, I have a very hard time selling it, but if I really like an item or product, I can sell it immediately to someone that had no intention of buying it. I wanted to find another business I could get very excited about.

Celebrity memorabilia was it! I loved important movie props and wardrobes from big films, historical documents, contracts, personal checks, and autographs of top celebrities in all fields: from vintage Hollywood to sports, politics, and history. I got very excited when I obtained awesome pieces of history like Thomas Edison's patent for the light bulb, a Babe Ruth homerun baseball, and Elvis Presley's purchasing contract to buy Graceland.

Unlike the traditional nine to five job with the same routine and same paycheck every week, I liked the unpredictability of my memorabilia business. You just don't know what's going to happen from week to week. It seems like every time things start to slow down, someone drops the collection of a lifetime in your lap.

Todd Mueller is a guy in our business who is always buying collections, large and small. One day I sent Todd a package of extra stuff I'd picked up in a deal that included a vintage original Desilu check signed by Lucille Ball, which had a book value of about $400. I offered it to him for $250. Todd laughed at me and said, "Haven't you heard about that collection floating around? A family member of the accountant from Desilu Productions has about 3,000 signed Lucy checks, a couple thousand Desi Arnez signed checks, signed contracts, scripts—all kinds of stuff. He wants $100,000 for the whole collection."

I did some quick figuring in my head. That would work out to about $17 per signature. "I'll take it," I said.

"What do you mean you'll take it? That collection has been passed up by a lot of big companies because it's so much stuff. It will flood the market, and the prices will go down," Todd explained

I knew *I Love Lucy* fans were worldwide. Hell, there's still a Lucille Ball Festival in Los Angeles every year. Lucy Ball is a top ten, all-time best celebrity. At that price the deal was a no-brainer. Who cares if the price goes down a bit as we sell them into the market? They'll NEVER go down to anywhere near what we're paying for them, plus it's not like Lucy and Desi are going to pop out of their graves to start signing anymore stuff.

"I want it," I told him.

I didn't care what anyone else in the business thought. I knew in my gut this was a good deal. Todd was in Texas, and it turned out the collection happened to be right in Los Angeles. I asked to have the contact if he wasn't buying it. He called me back a few hours later and said, "I'm going to take a chance with you Tom. Let's go partners on the deal and split it 50/50. Just don't sell them all over eBay and drive the pieces down."

I agreed that whoring the signed Lucy and Desi checks all over eBay was a bad idea. Instead I pre-sold a few hundred to some local dealers to cover my end of the deal. By the time I was done trading and selling off the rest of the collection, the huge profit we both made proved that I should always go with my gut instinct over the opinions of other big dealers. As a matter a fact, I sold lots of those Lucy checks to all the other companies who hadn't wanted the whole collection but were interested in lots of 50 or 100 checks at a much higher price than I'd paid.

Now it was official! I wasn't even out of prison for six months, and with the money I made from the Desilu deal, I paid back all the loans my brothers lent me while I was in prison. I had plenty of cash in the bank, a new thriving online business with lots of inventory, a happy reunited family, and a nice little house. I had the urge to go back to that quack of a prison psych who basically told me I was insane for even dreaming about everything I'd just obtained, but I knew it was best to stay as far away as I could from any parole administrators.

My life, like a rollercoaster, was great now that it was riding high; but like all great rides, my life was headed for yet another pitfall.

Chapter Sixteen

PAROLE VIOLATION
1998 - 1999

My family seemed complete living in our new house. I was never happier, but somehow I knew the joy couldn't last. We were in the house about a week when I was in the kitchen installing the refrigerator. Then all of a sudden, I heard a sharp BANG! BANG! BANG! on my front door. I opened the door, and there stood a little Mexican guy with a goatee. I was pissed off that he was making so much noise and shouted, "What do you want?"

He showed me his badge and informed me he was my new parole officer. I had moved out of the nice parole lady's district, and now I had this guy for my new parole agent. "What do I want? I'll show you what the fuck I want! Homie," he said. "Get up against the wall!" He frisked me down and interrogated me about who lived there with me, how I'd gotten the money to buy the house, and where I kept my drugs. He was harassing me.

"I don't do drugs and never have," I told him.

"You're a fucking liar," he said. It wasn't a great introduction. This new guy told me he was fine with a paroled murderer who lived down the street, but for some reason he hated me. As soon as he left, I got on the phone and unsuccessfully tried to get reassigned to my old parole officer.

He asked how I was making a living during his next visit. When I told him in memorabilia, he said I couldn't do it anymore. Since I had gotten in trouble dealing in collectibles before, he ordered me to find a new job at a fast food restaurant or something. I went to the supervisor of the parole office and explained how anything could be considered a collectable. As long as it's legal, it shouldn't be a problem. She agreed with me and overruled my parole agent by saying, "If you have the slightest problem in your business, you can be violated. But it's up to you. For now you can continue doing your work."

You have no rights as a parolee, and your parole agent can basically do whatever he wants. A few months later my little parole officer showed up at 5:00 a.m. for an unannounced visit and started rampaging through our house and tearing it apart. He found a little toy popgun my father-in-law had given my youngest daughter in her toy box. He immediately arrested me for "being a parolee in possession of simulated firearms."

"Try getting this charge overruled, Homes!" my gangsta parole agent laughed as he placed me in handcuffs. He brought me to the Long Beach detention center where they booked me for violating my parole and took that mug shot of me that everyone can see to this day on SmokingGun.com.

My parole officer recommended I serve a year in prison for this violation, but a bunch of my associates showed up at the hearing to support me. It touched me that they were just as outraged as I was.

The parole board was very tough; they all examined the apparently harmless toy gun in question and emphasized that it was my responsibility to keep anything like this out of my house. One of the women on the board told me a story about one of their parolees who had been doing very well for a couple years. It was a condition of his probation that he was not allowed to drink or keep alcohol in the house because of a previous DUI where he injured someone. His wife hired a workman to fix something, and the guy left a couple of beers in the refrigerator. The parole officer showed up that day and saw it, and the parolee went back to prison for a one-year violation. It was his responsibility to know what was in his refrigerator, and it was mine to know what was in my kids' toy box while I was on parole. You are not free when you're on parole. You are still very much in custody of the state.

Ninety-nine percent of the time the parole board in violation hearings simply does whatever the parole officer recommends. This time, because of my big show of support, they sentenced me to six months instead of a year. I went back to prison to serve six months, the first two in county jail (a very rough place if you're not gang-associated) and then all the way back to Avenol State Prison for the rest of my sentence. Avenol seemed like a walk in the park after the hellish time I spent in the L.A. County Jail, but this time I got through it easier knowing I had my wife and kids to go home to. I got out in four months with good behavior.

After I was released, my wife and I both showed up at the parole office. "Listen, you have got to reassign me to a different parole officer. This guy has made it clear he doesn't like me. I can't win! He's never gonna let up; you've got to reassign me." Thankfully they reassigned my case to a different officer who was very cool, and the rest of my three years on parole went smoothly.

Thank God, that was the last time I was ever in trouble with the law.

Chapter Seventeen

OPERATION BULLPEN
1999

The baseball card business had completely gone down the shitter. The card market was so different than what it had been just 10 years earlier. People used to bring in $20,000 collections and ask for $1,000. Now, they were bringing in $1,000 collections and asking for $20,000. The whole game just wasn't worth it anymore.

Hundreds of baseball card shops everywhere were folding faster than Superman on laundry day, but there was something bigger on the horizon: eBay. Thanks to my friend Lowell, I had one of the very first accounts on eBay. I opened it in 1997 and by 1999, it was becoming common knowledge that eBay was a less expensive and more convenient way of selling than running a neighborhood shop. You just needed to make sure that all your feedback scores were positive.

I'm very proud of the fact that to this day, after thousands of transactions, my member I.D. universalrarities still has 100 percent positive feedback and no negatives because I'm always willing to resolve matters for my customers. If the item got damaged in the mail or if it's not up to their expectations, whatever happens, I take full responsibility and fix it. I'll go above and beyond for customer service. A problem arises every 50 orders or so but that's business. Fix it, get past it, and count your money. That's my philosophy.

Lowell was a big help to me, but he seemed to be doing a lot of work on eBay for a small return. I said to him, "You know, you're doing a lot of work to put 100 cheap cards a day on eBay, and the auctions are closing at only 50¢ or $1 each. If you sold some $100 or $200 items, you'd spend the same amount of time listing them, but you'd make a much higher profit."

Lowell had seen how much money I made on my Desilu deal and started to look for similar deals. One day he called me and said, "I think I found the answer! I met this guy named Wayne at a card show this weekend. He has a really good source for autographs down in San Diego. I just bought a few to run on eBay."

Lowell sold the autographs on eBay and did well. The next thing I knew, he had hundreds of autographs and was making thousands of dollars a week selling them online. I was so jealous. I wanted to invest in his deal, but he wouldn't take me to his source.

After a while I stated getting a little suspicious: How many Babe Ruth and Marilyn Monroe autographs could one guy have? This wasn't like the big Desilu find where an accountant had a big undiscovered stash of signed checks and documents. This situation practically said, "Place your order Lowell. How many James Dean autographs do you need this week?"

It seemed strange, but the Certificate of Authenticity (COA) that came with each autograph set everybody's mind at ease. Lowell's connection, Wayne, always provided a COA from a company called the J. DiMaggio Company which for a short time was well respected in the hobby.

One day Lowell came over to my house, and I pleaded with him, "I know you won't take me down to deal with Wayne because he's your source for the autographs, but can I at least get some of my documents authenticated by this J. DiMaggio Company?"

"Okay," Lowell said, "I'm going there now. You can meet him and get your stuff authenticated."

We went to a Starbucks Coffee, and Lowell pointed him out. I walked up, held my hand out to him, and said, "So you're the famous J. DiMaggio! Any relation to Joe?"

It was like a scene from the old *Munsters* TV show when Marilyn Munster introduces her new boyfriend to her Uncle Herman. This guy's eyes popped out in fear, and then he ran out of that place so fast I thought I saw smoke kick up as he turned the corner. "What the hell Lowell?" I asked.

"Maybe he's a little shy," Lowell guessed.

It was obvious that this "DiMaggio" guy was spooked by me because he was a paranoid fraud who thought I was another person from the media trying to expose him as the impostor he was. Soon people started questioning DiMaggio's creditability after an article appeared stating that he was just a restaurant owner who had absolutely no credentials to be an autograph examiner, and he was intentionally misleading people by letting them think that Joe DiMaggio was involved with his authentication company.

J. DiMaggio suddenly disappeared and up popped Donald Frangipani. All of the new autographs in town came complete with Donald Frangipani's COA, and this really seemed like great news because it was quickly confirmed that Frangipani was a federal court recognized forensic expert.

Donald Frangipani is a very important figure in the history of the collectibles business. He worked for many years with the federal government as a forensic handwriting expert and testified in countless trials. His testimony helped put dozens of accused forgers behind bars. He had his own business authenticating autographs and seemed like an impeccable source to use. He listed his phone number on his COA, so I called him up and started steering all my business his way.

I was surprised at how many things he passed. I would buy collections contingent that they pass his inspection and sent them to him thinking that some were secretarial signatures or just not authentic, but he'd pass almost all of them. Every once in a great while, he'd tell me something was a copy and not an actual signature, just a preprint or something like that, but those occasions were rare. Maybe 1 item in a 100 he'd fail or say it was inconclusive.

One day a package came in the mail. I opened it, and to my surprise, there was the most amazing signed card collection I've ever seen. Hundreds of vintage superstar signed baseball cards of everyone from Ruth to Mantle. The cards alone had to be worth about $100,000. The package was from Donald Frangipani's office. I called him right away and returned the package. I was even more surprised when other dealers told me they had similar experiences. This guy didn't seem to have it together, but at the time Frangipani was the number one authenticator on eBay, and any item certified by him sold for a great deal of money.

Donald was a nice old man from Brooklyn, and he invited me to visit his office when I went back east to see my parents. I accepted and found him to be a very talkative Italian guy in his sixties. He had microscopes as big as my daughter all over his forensic lab. He was happy to give demonstrations about how certain inks bled into certain papers and other forensic facts that were very interesting to me. Letters of commendation from people like U.S. Attorney General Janet Reno, thanking him for his excellent work putting criminals behind bars, hung on his walls. Bottom line, no one in the world seemed more qualified to authenticate an autograph than Donald Frangipani, and if my government hires him to examine their questioned documents, so should I. I liked the guy personally, I trusted him, and I felt safe using him at the time.

Things were going well, and one day Lowell stopped by and said, "You know Tom, I was speaking to Wayne today, and your name came up. He really wants to meet you, and I gave my permission as long as you don't go around me to make deals with him. If you make a deal with him, I want 10 percent whether I'm there or not. Agreed?"

"Okay," I said, and Lowell took me to see Wayne.

The ride was about two hours all the way down by San Diego. We got there, and to my surprise, a seedy looking guy with tattoos all over comes out to shake my hand.

"Tom Riccio! Everywhere I go I hear your name, and now I finally get to meet you. My name is Wayne Bray."

"Hi Wayne, I've heard a lot about you," I said, "I hope we can do a lot of business."

Just then Wayne drops about a dozen vintage looking Babe Ruth autographs on the table and says I can have them all at $50 each.

"Wow!" I yelled, "You were making some big profits on me Lowell!"

Lowell looked confused. "You never sold me stuff like this so cheap," he said

"We just got a big shipment in, and we need to move it all. Don't worry Lowell, there's plenty more for you," Wayne confirmed.

"Okay, I'll take them all if you have the Frangipani COAs with them, and can you give me a receipt so I can show they were bought legitimately?" I always asked for receipts at that point while I was on parole, in case something turned up stolen.

Wayne laughed kind of nervously, "Come on Tom, COAs from Frangipani? That guy is a quack; every crook uses him to get their forgeries passed. He doesn't know a Mickey Mantle autograph from a Mickey Mouse autograph!"

"So, what are you saying Wayne?" I wanted the bottom line.

"Do you really think you're getting real Babe Ruth autographs for only $50 each? Of course these are all forgeries!"

"Wayne, I've gotten great deals legally on a lot of things in my business. It's not the price that ever concerns me, but if you are telling me that you think these things are forgeries, I don't want them at any price!"

We got the hell out of there, and Lowell said he didn't understand why Wayne said all that shit. Lowell said he believed that the stuff he'd bought up to that point was real. I told him to be careful dealing with that Bray character, and we went home without buying a thing on our trip.

One thing Wayne Bray said turned out to be fact: Federal court recognized forensic expert Donald Frangipani turned out to be a quack. James Spence of JSA Authentication even called him Donald Duck. I started to reconsider using him all the time, but I liked him as a person and was sure 99 percent of the stuff I was sending him was real anyway. Then word leaked out among the hobby that Frangipani was so incompetent that all the forgers sent him stuff knowing he would pass them. He certainly wasn't in cahoots with any forgers or anything like that, but he clearly was no longer competent. He just passed almost everything anyone sent him.

A week or so later, Lowell calls me crying, "The FBI came to my house, took all my inventory, and arrested me for dealing in forged items!"

I shouted, "Holy shit, Lowell!" I remembered that I gave Lowell about $10,000 worth of space lithographs to sell on eBay that had nothing to do with his Wayne Bray deals.

"Did the FBI take all my signed space lithos along with your fake shit?" I asked.

"Yes, they took EVERYTHING!" Lowell told me, "You can call this FBI guy Tim Fitzsimmons. He's the guy who took your real stuff along with the fakes I bought from Wayne. Here's his phone number. Maybe he'll give you your stuff back."

I called Agent Fitzsimmons at the San Diego FBI, and he sounded pissed off at me. "Are you kidding Mr. Riccio! You are not getting a single piece of your stuff back whether it's real or not. Sue your buddy Lowell Katz, but you won't get it from us!" Then to my shock, he said, "You are so lucky you didn't buy any of those Babe Ruth autographs at Bray's place that day. We were hoping so bad that you'd buy just one so we could lock you up!"

I almost pissed my pants! That place down in San Diego was bugged by the FBI while that fucking Wayne Bray guy tried to set us up! FBI Agent Fitzsimmons went on scolding me, "If I were you Mr. Riccio, I'd get into a different line of work, because I know all about your past. I see more trouble in your future if you don't quit this field of work." Hmm, maybe Agent Fitzsimmons was psychic.

Lowell was just a small part of a huge FBI sting called "Operation Bullpen." This was actually a great idea where the Feds decided to crack down on all the phony autographs in the business. The Marinos, a family of artists who doubled in forgery, were putting out thousands of forged autographs. Most of them ended up at Donald Frangipani's office to get authenticated, and he'd passed almost all of them. These forgers/artists would sell them though their sleazy broker Wayne Bray, Wayne would flip them cheap to dealers, and the dealers would resell them to customers worldwide.

The Marinos got caught, then the dealers got squeezed, and everybody started turning on everybody else. I'm sure some of these dealers were in on it, but I know that a lot of them bought the autographs in good faith thinking if they came with Frangipani certification they must be real.

The Feds went after all the dealers and wound up making deals consisting of fines and probation with most of those who were caught. About 10 million dollars in cash and property were seized. The bottom line is many dealers paid to have their items authenticated by an FBI expert, sold them in good faith, and then were prosecuted for it. A few of them refused to bow down and waited for their day in court.

The biggest issue I have is why in the world would the FBI make deals with the Marino Family of forgers and their main broker Wayne Bray just to set up dozens of dealers nationwide? For most of the year, the FBI was basically ordering Wayne Bray to sell FAKE autographs into the hobby so they can get more dealers involved and obtain more indictments. Meanwhile the FBI facilitated the fraud against thousands of innocent collectors worldwide who bought these fake items on eBay and elsewhere. I've met a lot of these customers who were scammed by the FBI and think Fitzsimmons and the FBI should at the very least take that 10 million they seized from the dealers and give it back to the innocent customers they defrauded in their sting.

I have had a few friends tell me to watch what I say in this book, because if the wrong person reads it, the FBI or the IRS could make life very hard on me. However, I made a promise to my publisher that I would tell them all the facts as I saw them, and if that brings on some kind of wrath from any authorities, then there's something wrong with us as a society. We live in America and not 1940s fascist Germany!

The main issue with Operation Bullpen is most of the dealers used Donald Frangipani to authenticate the autographs in question. They felt the item must be authentic because the FBI's own expert passed them, but the FBI would say, "You knew this Frangipani guy was an incompetent!"

An arrested dealer would respond, "Really, then why did *you* use him?" That would shut the FBI up real quick, and the person charged would get offered a deal they thought they couldn't refuse.

If one of the dealers had enough nerve to actually show up in court and say, "I got all my items authenticated by Donald Frangipani, and the Feds said he was incompetent as a Forensic expert," what would that mean for the dozens of people who were sent to prison by the FBI on his expert testimony? If this information were ever made public, they would have to retry everyone. There would be lawsuits!

There was one father/son dealer team I knew who was facing decades in prison and millions in fines for selling fake autographs, interstate travel—you name it. They piled up the charges on them and said, "We'll offer you five years and a $50,000 fine." However, the father and son weren't interested and were furiously holding out for their day in court.

"Okay, okay, probation for Dad and six months in a federal camp for the son," the prosecutor said. Due to their rising legal costs, the father and son took the deal. Still, I'm sure the Feds weren't going to let anyone go to court and reveal that their star autograph-expert witness had been exposed as a quack.

Most everyone in the hobby stayed away from his office like the plague, but Frangipani was stubborn and continued to sell his Signature Verification service to the autograph hobby. The word started to get around, business slowed down, and anything with his seal was worthless.

It didn't make sense to do business with Frangipani after that. I didn't speak with him for a while, and then about a year later, a customer came in with a small collection of autographed figures he'd obtained in person. He asked for Frangipani to authenticate it, and I sent it to him. I called him after a week. "Hey, Donald did you get that package of signed toys?"

"Yes," said Frangipani. "Tim Fitzsimmons was here and said you are friends with Lowell Katz from Operation Bullpen, so I'm sending your stuff back. It's all no good."

That was a few years ago and the last time anyone ever asked me for Frangipani's services. EBay and just about every auction house in the world refuses to accept any items with his examination letters and several TV shows have done exposés on Frangipani including HBO's *Real Sports*.

In episode 106 of *Real Sports*, which originally aired on January 17, 2006, *Real Sports* quoted the FBI saying they used an "authenticator of choice"—a licensed forensic expert from Brooklyn named Donald Frangipani for the ring.

I was told that the person appearing on the show under a pseudonym was actually Shelly Jaffe who was convicted in the FBI's Operation Bullpen sting. Jaffe claimed, "The only reason this forgery ring worked is we were able to find forensic experts."

The reporter said, "Frangipani was never charged with any involvement in the forgery ring. In fact, he's still doing business today." So, *Real Sports* reporters posed as customers and arrived at Frangipani's office with seven known forged items and a hidden camera.

Frangipani examined the seven forged signatures and provided seven certificates of authenticity. He ironically warned the group, "This stuff is good, but you don't know what you are going to come across out there. There's a lot of bad stuff." *Real Sports* later returned to Frangipani's office and informed him that the signatures he'd certified as genuine were actually forgeries. Frangipani tried to claim he was merely providing his opinion, "If these are items that I passed and they're known to be fake, again, I gave an opinion on these items."

The reporter also asked Frangipani if he ever became suspicious with the huge shipments of items with signatures he received, "I'm just curious...when you get all these items coming in...you don't say at some point and time, what the hell's going on here? Where's all this stuff coming from? How can there be this much real stuff out there?"

A book entitled *Operation Bullpen* by Kevin Nelson was written about the FBI sting. Although Nelson mentions how some forgers copied Frangipani's COAs to put with their forgeries, he never mentioned that Frangipani was working as an expert witness for the FBI while the forgery ring used his services to pass their forgeries!

On January 19, 2008, I got a hold of *Bullpen* author Kevin Nelson by phone and he told me he thought FBI agent Tim Fitzsimmons was a "straight shooter" who did what he had to do to get all the fake autographs off the market—even if some innocent customers had to be scammed until it was done. Nelson seemed to be a very sincere professional reporter, but I still can't figure out why he never mentioned that Donald Frangipani was an FBI expert witness while he was passing fake items for a forgery ring. When I asked Nelson about that, he kept saying, "Read the book. Everything I knew is in the book. If that is not mentioned in there, then I didn't know about it."

It's been so many years since I've spoken with Frangipani and thought people would want to know if he's still in business. What the hell, I decided, and called Frangipani's office number on the very same day. Don answered, "Investigations!" There was no mistaking that raspy Peter Falk-type voice of his. It brought me right back to all our old conversations. It was just like going back to the 1990s.

"Hi Donald, it's Tom Riccio," I replied.

At first he seemed glad to hear from me but then said, "Hey Tom! I saw you on TV with the O.J. tape. Are you recording me?"

"No Donald, but I'm writing a book, and I wanted to ask you some questions."

Right away he got all defensive. I guess he figured my book wasn't *The World's Greatest Forensic Experts*. He told me he had been a forensic examiner for more than 30 years, but he wasn't God and makes mistakes. He only gives opinions. He also reminded me that some cheap forgers took his original COAs and made copies to put with forgeries that he never even examined. It still doesn't take away the fact that he did pass thousands of autographs that both the FBI and collectors worldwide now know to be forgeries.

Then he said something that amazed me, "I'm over 70 years old now, and I still work as a court forensic expert witness for the government." Everyone knows the inaccuracy of his conclusions, yet somehow he's still working as an FBI court forensic expert where his opinions could ruin someone's life forever!

"Donald, it's one thing when you mess up on an autograph opinion, but aren't you concerned about screwing up a critical opinion in court which might affect someone's life and get them unjustly sent to prison?" I asked.

Frangipani became enraged, "You better not say anything bad about me in your book, or I'll call Agent Tim Fitzsimmons on you so fast you'll think it's 1999."

I believe it's my obligation to somehow get this information out there. If I save just one person from getting their life ruined over his suspect forensic testimony, I'll feel like I've accomplished something.

* * *

I had to find another company for authentications. A new company called PSA/DNA out of Santa Ana, California, was legitimate and publicly traded, but their name created what I'd call one of the biggest misconceptions in the business. Several times I would have an item, and a customer would say to me, "Tom, I'll take it, but you need to get DNA for it."

"What do you mean DNA?"

"You need to send it to this company PSA/DNA. They run a big DNA test on every item, right?"

"You've got to be kidding! You think they do a $20,000 DNA test? No! A guy looks at it, examines it, and says it's good or it's not good...puts the sticker on or doesn't. That's it!" Their trick is to swab every item they examine with a pen containing synthetic DNA and then put on a sticker. All that means is that they looked at it; they didn't run a DNA test on it! They employ competent authenticators and err on the side of caution. If they think there's even a 10 percent chance the item may not be real, they won't pass it and will charge you either way (most authenticators don't charge for items they don't pass).

Everyone is bamboozled by their name. It's hard for me to believe so many people think they're getting a DNA test for $50, but there you have it. This company has more business than they can handle. They're number one in the business, and when you're number one, you don't have to treat your customers with great service.

According to the Autograph Business News and Notes website, PSA/DNA has been flunked by the Better Business Bureau. "The Better Business Bureau of Southern California has now given PSA an F rating," the website stated. "That is the lowest possible rating that a company can get from the BBB."

The website quoted the BBB's reasoning for the poor rating: "Some complainants allege the company fails to return items sent in for authentication, and in some cases deny ever receiving the item...items sent are lost, misplaced.... Customers report they experience difficulties contacting the company to resolve problems, calls are not returned, and voicemail or e-mail messages are not answered."

As long as PSA/DNA keeps their ingenious name, they'll probably always be number one—even with their new authenticators coming and going, even with all the bad press, even with all the complaints, and maybe even if they hired Donald Frangipani to authenticate for them on the down-low.

Chapter Eighteen

SILLY CDs
2000 - 2002

The tremendous luck I had in my youth made me believe that gambling was the answer to any problem, but I'm older now and not 25. I know it's not smart to count on a bet in times of need. Business is a different story because when I gamble in business, 95 percent of the time I win. When I had the opportunity to start my own card company in November 2000, I went for it.

I had to face the fact that the card market, as far as new cards are concerned, died around 1994. Old classic baseball cards will always have a market, but the new card companies like Fleer and Donruss went out of business. There were only two major card manufacturers left, Topps and Upper Deck, and even they were considering merging. A couple events in the past decade like Pokémon cards were a real craze among kids for a while, but the days of the can't-miss card series were gone. A successful new series was a long shot at best.

I remembered the feeling of buying Wacky Packs when I was a kid in the 1970s. I couldn't get enough of them. My friends and I traded them with each other. Wacky Packs were funny parody cards with great art that made fun of products. For example, "Wheaties—Breakfast of Champs" became "Weakees—Breakfast of Chumps." I loved them! When I became an adult I noticed that the original art from Wacky Packs became very valuable. Topps had sold their archives of original art for a couple hundred dollars each. When the Internet became widely used, young adults who remembered collecting Wacky Packs started buying old

Wacky Packs cards and original art. A print of the original art could go for as much as $20,000. I started dealing in the art and found out that a couple of the artists (Jay Lynch and John Pound) were still alive. They were also the same geniuses who invented Garbage Pail Kids and sold millions of these items in the 1980s. I contacted them to see if they had any more original art, but Topps had taken all of it.

"Why don't we do a new series of Wacky Packs?" I asked.

"We can't," Jay explained, "Topps owns the rights to the name and series, but we could do something different."

I thought about a number of different things. I considered Silly Cinema where they'd do spoofs of famous movie posters like *The Exorcist*. We went so far as to come up with prototypes for a series called Tacky TV with such shows like *The Osbournes* becoming *The Ozzbutts*, but at the last minute, Jay, John, and I agreed that record or CD covers were the best things to parody because kids like music more than anything else. I came up with the name "Silly CDs," and we came up with some prototypes. They were fun but not edgy enough.

Michael Jackson Silly CDs parody card

"Let's push the envelope a little more," I urged Jay. Jay did one for Michael Jackson's *Bad* with "Michael Jackass—*Sad*" making fun of all his well-publicized troubles. The caricature of Michael Jackson had his nose falling off and little boys crawling all over him. It was a riot! Whitney Houston became "Witless Houston," Elton John became "Two-ton John," and the Doors became "the Dorks." My favorite Silly CD card was a parody of the Beatles' *Abbey Road* because it was me in the VW Bug screaming at the Beatles as they walked across Abbey Road.

People kept warning us that we were going to get sued, but we knew that the satire was perfectly legal.

I was really happy when Garth Brooks agreed to pose with me and his Silly CDs parody which he thought was hilarious.

Furthermore, all the stars were into them. I have pictures of Justin Timberlake, Garth Brooks, and Gene Simmons posing with their cards. They loved them, and when we sent them to publicists, they always called back looking for more. *Mad* and *Cracked* magazines, both of which I'd loved as a kid, were anxious to feature a new card each month. I wound up doing a deal with *Cracked*, and they featured an interview with me describing how I put it all together.

We took Silly CDs to the New York Toy Show, and out of 50,000 entries, we were voted the number 7 toy that year. Silly CDs was also named Playthings Toy of the Week, and the high point was when a representative from the Target chain signed on to carry Silly CDs nationwide in their 1,000 stores.

We were offered the best production cost if we printed 5,000 cases with each case containing 12 boxes of cards. Each box had 24 packs of cards which could be sold separately. We were excited about the Target order and ordered 5,000 cases.

Back in the late 80s and early 90s, that many cases would have been a realistic number, but most card series consisted of 200 to 300 cases by 2001. Looking back, our optimism was unrealistic. As we were anxiously awaiting the product to be delivered, I was floored when I heard that Silly CDs cards were all over eBay! How could that be? We hadn't even seen them yet! It turned out the eBay seller lived in the same town where our printing company was located. An employee from the printers had stolen a few cases and put them on eBay before the boxes even left the printing factory.

The printing company totally denied that one of their employees would commit such a crime. No matter how much I tried to point out that our cards were obviously stolen from

Spice Girls Silly CDs parody card

Madonna Silly CDs parody card

their factory, because our series was up for sale on eBay for $5 a set and undercutting our price of $1.99 per single pack before we'd ever even received the product. Why should anyone now pay retail from us? I was frustrated and did some investigating; I found out the seller's name. Sure enough, he worked in shipping at the printing company. Even when I called the president of the company back with the guy's name, he denied everything up and down. "It doesn't necessarily mean that the John McCauley who's selling your stolen product on eBay is the same John McCauley that works for us," he said. I couldn't believe they were trying to deny this obvious leak in their security.

All of this nonsense barely detracted from my excitement about Silly CDs. On my birthday in 2001, I was attending my ITEX barter trade show, and somebody told me that Silly CDs were out in Target. I stopped by the Target next to the show and saw my Silly CDs on the rack at $1.99 a pack. A couple of teenagers were looking at them. "Look," one of the kids said laughing, "The Lice Girls!" It was one of the happiest and proudest moments of my life. The feeling of something I had invented being sold in a big nationwide store chain was such a thrill I can't put it into words.

The first week we received pretty strong sales reports. Quite a few of the boxes had sold out and many stores only had a few packs left. They were right on the fence of the large re-order we were hoping for, but sales dropped way off the second week. When I saw that report, it felt like my heart was being torn out of my chest. The third week was even worse than the second week. What had happened?

We soon found out. After the first week's sales, the store's inventory showed that some of these Targets had 10 packs left or so, but no more sales were recorded after that because there weren't any more packs to sell. Kids were stealing all the packs and walking out of the stores. The individual packs were small and easy to steal. It's what store management referred to as a "loss prevention problem," but it wasn't really their problem. According to the contract, they were not responsible for any lost or stolen inventory.

It was explained to me that Target didn't have the personnel to put the cards in a glass case and spend a lot of time locking and unlocking the case and monitoring kids. I was told we had to repackage the cards in a blister pack with a security tag to make it more difficult to walk out of the

Barney the Dinosaur Silly CDs parody card

store with them. They weren't going to reorder more unless we complied, but that would've doubled our costs. We couldn't do it and were out of Target.

Buyers from Wal-Mart were still interested. The younger staff absolutely loved them, but we hit a wall at the top levels of management when the older decision makers did not see the humor in Barney the Dinosaur parody cards like "Barfey the Wino-saur." They also didn't know who Britney Spears was and didn't care. The upper management wouldn't sign off on the barf and bathroom humor in the cards.

I had kids and was still a kid at heart. I knew that kids love boogers and fart jokes and stuff like that—the grosser the better. However, it's not funny when you're a 70-year-old CEO. It's tacky. This scenario repeated itself at K-Mart. We were never able to get Silly CDs into a big chain again. We wound up selling a couple hundred more cases here and there, but I was left with a warehouse full of about 4,000 cases of cards. That's a lot of leftover inventory!

Our investors were furious that we'd lost the Target deal—and basically our shirts. They placed the loss squarely on the printer of the cards for letting the product get stolen on their watch, sold on eBay at a fraction of its list price, and therefore ruining their perceived value. After an internal investigation, the printer finally admitted that their employee had stolen the cards and put them up for sale on eBay. They fired the guy and denied all liability by stating that it wasn't within his job description to steal our product.

Elton John Silly CDs parody card

Whitney Houston Silly CDs parody card

Willie Nelson Silly CDs parody card

According to our projected forecasts, sales could have been $2.8 million. Since that didn't happen, we sued the printer for $2.8 million. After a great deal of wrangling back and forth for the next year and a half, our lawyers backed out a couple of days before the trial. They had taken the case on contingency and weren't anxious to travel to another state 2,000 miles away for a trial. I got on the phone with the owner of the printing company, and he said, "We know the situation was very distressing to you, but come on, $2.8 million? Give me a realistic number, and we'll settle this right now."

"Well, you can reimburse me for all the printing costs for starters," I said. That was more than $200,000 right there.

"One hundred thousand dollars cash," he said.

"Two hundred thousand," I countered. "I have investors, we lost business...."

"I have my people on this, and we are prepared to go to trial. It would probably cost me less to take this to trial. So this is my final offer: $150,000. Take it or leave it."

Since our lawyers bailed before the settlement, it didn't cost us a penny in legal fees. My partner and I agreed to take the offer. We paid back our investors: $100,000 to one and $50,000 to the other. I wound up with the remaining

Snoop Dogg Silly CDs parody card

Tupac Shakur Silly CDs parody card

4,000 cases of Silly CD cards, the rights to all of the original art, and all the patent and licensing rights to the series forever, but as far as cash goes, I got zip. It turned out alright because I got a decent deal to use the cards with a bubble gum company and a candy bar deal. Some money started coming in, but the card sales themselves were dead. It was costing me money to store all those cases, so I went out to look for a licensing agent to make more deals to use my Silly CD images on other products.

I e-mailed three licensing agents images of my Silly CDs. Two replied back with interest. One licensing company was very big, and the other was a small individual agent named Bob Stein of the Grove Group.

The big company was kind of warm on the idea of picking up Silly CDs as a client and told me, "We'll show it around and see how it goes for a few months."

Bob Stein was unstoppable. "Tom, these cards are hilarious! I loved Wacky Packages as a kid, and I think your series is even better. I'd really appreciate it if I could get an opportunity to represent your series." That was all I needed to hear and signed on with Bob Stein.

About a week later Bob calls me about two companies interested in a T-Shirt deal. One of them also wanted to use my Silly CDs on pajamas and boxer shorts. The offers were for a $10,000 advance and 10 percent of sales for each agreement. Ten grand was about the normal advance, and I told him to accept the deal for the pajamas and shorts but hold off for a better deal for the T-shirts. A day later Bob calls and said, "This company called Exquisite Apparel would not take no for an answer on the T-shirts, so I sold them the rights."

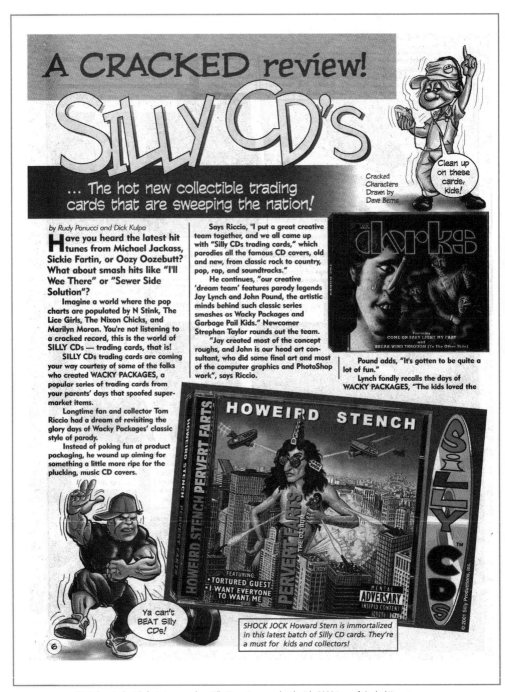

This is the actual article featuring me and my Silly CDs as it appeared in the July 2002 Issue of *Cracked* Magazine.

Wackies, and the kids'll love the Silly CDs too . . . I think the CD gags have that same old sense of stupidity to them.

"Tom picked the subjects. He tried to hit all ages and all tastes."

Says Riccio, "This is the first parody series that targets both kids and adults, with spoofs of classic artists like The Doors and The Beatles to new pop acts such as Britney Spears and N SYNC."

SILLY CDs treat us to such classics as NO TROUT's "Just a Churl", THE BACKWASH BOYS' "We've Got It Goin' On Us", and THE DORKS' "Come On Baby, Light My Fart".

You really have to admire Riccio's perseverance in seeing this project through. It's not easy calling someone "Bruce Stinkjeans", and getting away with it.

"Of course there were, and are, and will continue to be problems with getting a project like this off the ground."

Riccio adds, "but like anything you really believe in, you move forward and go for it, which I have."

The series is now selling in the hobby market, as well as retail outlets like pharmacies, department stores and music stores.

A bubbly Riccio tells us that his distributors are placing hundreds of orders daily.

They're selling for a measly $1.99

These babies are 'tight on'!

per pack, with three title cards and two puzzle pieces in each package. There are 33 title cards and 6 different six-piece puzzles to collect.

Inserted in one of every four packs will be one of 11 different sticker versions of the cards.

Future sets may include "chase" cards autographed by the creative team.

The backs of the cards will feature card numbers, checklists, and information on SILLY CD merchandise.

SILLY CDs are already having a huge impact on the music scene, just like the day Bob Dylan quit taking singing lessons, or when Michael Jackson's nose changed.

Years from now, you'll want to say you were there, the day the music farted.

Cracked Magazine publisher Dick Kulpa loved the cards so much he traded this space for a free full collection.

Plus, he adds, the colorful art mixed in with some very creative spoofing fuels another dandy feature to entertain fellow Cracked-heads with.

For more info, check out www.sillycds.com!

It's time for Silly SIMPY CDs!

Everyone would hate those, Simpy!

CRACKED KICKS LID OFF PLOT TO SELL CHEAPER SNEAKERS!

ROCKFORD, ILL — A parents' group trying to talk kids into buying less-hip $19.95 tennis shoes gave up last week after Cracked advice columnist Butch Byteme cornered a local drug dealer and gently demonstrated the capabilities of his new $125 azz-kickers on the bad guy's butt.

For his actions, grateful parents honored Cracked's toughest mascot with a pair of bronzed Nikes!

"Oh yeah Bob, how much did you get for me?" I asked.

Bob screamed, "One hundred thousand dollars!"

I loved Bob Stein.

The company sold the T-shirts to a mall store named Spencer's Gift Store. The first title they made was a Britney Spears T-Shirt titled "Spitney Beers." Each store got only four T-shirts, and they all sold out in days. When they were asked to re-order, they were told that some moms had a problem with the parody and complained that the T-shirt that shows a young pop star puking up beer was very inappropriate. This was about Britney Fricking Spears and not Mother Teresa! So a store that literally sells "Farts in a Spray Can" pulled the funny Silly CD parody T-shirts and decided not to make anymore due to image concerns. That sucked, but at least I got to keep my $100,000 to console me!

I'm very proud of Silly CDs, and the fact that we sold over 1,000 cases in the "Dead Card Era" of the past 10 years. People are still discovering Silly CDs at close-out prices on eBay, and I still get e-mails from fans who tell me how much they love them and are hoping for a new series to come out. Another great thing I accomplished with Silly CDs was that they gave new life to the brilliant artists from Wacky Packs. That whole team was basically out of business for 15 years, and now they're back in the game because of exposure from Silly CDs. Topps paid them well for original artwork they did on a new series of Garbage Pail Kids and a new version of Wacky Packs.

I didn't think I'd be a part of something like that again, but I got a call from a card company called Breygent who was interested in buying some of the signed Lucille Ball checks I had to place in a new card series of *I Love Lucy* trading cards. I sold him a couple dozen checks. Their series sold 100 cases, and a few months later, I got another call. "I'd like to do another card series. I loved your Silly CD series. Maybe we can do something together?"

I told him I'm a big *Wizard of Oz* fan and actually owned an original brick from the Yellow Brick Road. They are very rare because most of the Yellow Brick Road was painted on in the film set. There were only a few actual yellow bricks. I had also done a deal in the past where I

purchased thousands of Jack Haley checks from the Tin
Man's grandson and had lion hair from the Cowardly
Lion Costume.

Breygent and I decided to go into business together
and start tracking down any of the Munchkins who might
still be alive to sign autographs on the cards. The yellow
brick, the checks I owned, and various other memorabilia
were no problem, but a card series had to be loaded with
extras to make them collectible. So, I set out to get
permission from Sid Luft to place Garland's signature on the
Oz cards.

Sid Luft was Garland's ex-husband and handled the
Judy Garland estate. I spoke to his son Joey on the phone
about the possibility of buying some of Garland's signed
checks. He told me they had some left and wanted to sell
them for $500 each, about $100 more per check than market
value. I told him I'd buy 10 if he would give us permission to
use them in a card series, and we settled on $5,000 for 10
signed Judy Garland checks plus permission to use them in
the card series.

Then Joey called back and said that his father was
scheduled for minor surgery so we should have this meeting
before he went to the hospital because it might take him a
long time to recover at his age. I went to his home/office, a
beautiful condo building in Santa Monica, and met the Lufts.
Sid was 90 years old when I met him, getting around in a
motorized scooter and perhaps just a touch senile. Everyone
warned me that Sid Luft was a miserable old fuck who was
impossible to deal with. I was expecting the worst, but he
was actually kind of nice to me. He told me he had Judy's
birth certificate, diploma, and all kinds of things. "Maybe it's
time to just get rid of all this stuff," he said.

"If you want to sell them, I'd appreciate the opportunity to place them in my next auction," I said, "I'm sure I
could get you top dollar." We signed the contract and I went
on my way.

Two days later while watching the E! Channel, the
scroll at the bottom of the screen reads, "90-year-old
producer and ex-husband of Judy Garland died today in
Santa Monica, California." I couldn't believe it! If I hadn't

gotten that signature, I couldn't have gone ahead with the *Wizard of Oz* card series.

It was onto the Munchkins, and they were not easy to deal with. Even though all of them were in their eighties and nineties, they still had large egos. Each and every one of them believed they were the most important part of the movie and wanted to be paid more than the others to sign our cards. We had to be scrupulously careful to pay them all exactly the same amount. Most of them said, "I had a much bigger part than him. I should get more!" It took careful

Me with munchkin Meinhardt Raabe who played "The Coroner" in the *Wizard of Oz*. Raabe signed cards for my *Wizard of Oz* card series.

negotiating, but I managed to sign all nine surviving Munchkins and put their autographs on the Oz cards.

After Silly CDs I wasn't expecting much, but this Oz series did very well. We sold around 250 cases of the first series of *Wizard of Oz* cards in about a month. They were one of the most popular series of the past 10 years. Then we produced a series of wooden boxes containing 10 packs of the cards, and they sold out in about a week. We were planning a third series with signature cards of Debbie Reynolds and her actual Ruby slippers from the film, but Turner Broadcasting was getting difficult to deal with and stalled us until our license ran out. So after two successful series, we just did like Dorothy—clicked our heels together and went home.

Chapter Nineteen

MORE ABOUT FAMILY
2003 - 2004

I was doing well and our family outgrew our small home in Long Beach, so as 2003 came to an end, we moved to a new larger house in Los Angeles. Our daughters were very happy to finally have their own rooms.

My teenage daughters are very unique in their own ways, but they both are similar in one respect: If either daughter wants to do something, she won't be denied.

My youngest daughter Clairissa at a recent 2008 modeling photo shoot.

Clairissa recently got her permit to drive and wanted to get a car. "Get a job," I said, stealing that line from my parents. Clair saw an ad for Angel Jeans where they were looking for a new unknown girl to represent their clothing line and decided to try out for that job.

"It's not that easy Clair, but why not?" I said. She went into the casting call with literally hundreds of other girls, and after a couple of call-backs, she got the job! She's now "The Angel Jeans Girl," with billboards featuring Clair in several countries around the world.

My oldest daughter Angela is also amazing. When I was in prison for three years, my asshole brother-in-law told Angie that her father was a low life convict, and she should be ashamed to be associated with me. An eight-year-old is very easily influenced, and I was worried that she would be embarrassed. After I was finally released from prison, I took Angela to the video store where she saw a group of her third grade friends. She ran up to her school friends and with a big smile on her face announced, "That's MY DADDY! He just got out of jail, and he's here to stay!" Angie was obviously proud to be my daughter, and I don't think I ever felt as blessed as I did at that moment. Angela also became an entertainment reporter at age 11. We live in Southern California, close to Hollywood, and it wasn't hard to send Angie to all kinds of entertainment events. The newspaper sent her to lots of local charity events and premieres where she interviewed all kinds of big stars from Mariah Carey to Jennifer Lopez to Mike Myers. Her articles were a local hit. The high point of Angie's writing career was at age 15 when she won the prestigious Young Artist Award for being the world's best teenage entertainment reporter. This time she was the one walking the red carpet with all the young stars while other reporters interviewed her. She looked better than any of the other beautiful starlets, and I was very proud when the paparazzi shouted my daughter's name as they snapped her picture at the award show.

Angie's weekly entertainment articles were very pop-

My daughter Angela with Elvis Presley's Grandson, Ben Keough.

ular, and she became friends with a lot of interesting people. One day she was covering a concert by Lisa Marie Presley and met her son Ben. He used to call Angie all the time, but one day his mom got on the phone and said, "Ben who are you talking to?"

Angie introduced herself, "Hi, I'm Angela, the teenage reporter who met Ben at your concert."

"REPORTER? Hang up the phone now Ben!" Lisa Marie screamed. The line went dead, and that was the last Angie ever heard of Ben. For some reason, most celebrities would rather hang out with an axe murderer than a reporter.

Angie got the feeling that reporters in Hollywood are welcomed like the plague. She lost her fascination with her job because of that and soon quit.

Like everyone else, I have many great stories and could probably write 10 books about my big Italian family. We've experienced good times and bad, but when you consider the large size of our family, I think it's amazing that for the most part we've all been blessed with incredible luck and health. That is until February 22, 2003.

I went home to Jersey to attend a family wedding and my 17-year-old nephew Carl invited me over to sit at his table. Carl was a fantastic athlete, over 6' tall, and good looking. Not only was he one of the top wrestlers in the state of New Jersey going 26-0 that year, Carl was also a heavily recruited baseball player. A lot of scouts were paying attention to him.

"Uncle Tommy," he told me. "I know you work with professional players to sell their autographs. If I get to the big leagues, I'll sign autographs for you for free!"

"Thanks Carl, you don't have to sign for free, but I'd love to represent you, and I'll make you money by getting lots of good signings and publicity."

"Hey, I remember all the baseball cards you used to give me when I was a kid. I'm telling you, I'll sign for free." My nephew is a great kid. A few weeks after our discussion, Carl had a wrestling match, and his opponent pulled some weird move on him. In a freak accident, Carl broke his neck and is now a quadriplegic, paralyzed from the neck down. The whole family was and still is devastated.

Here's the amazing thing: Carl still has the same outlook on life he always did. He goes to college and leads as normal a life as possible. After intensive therapy he regained enough movement in one arm to navigate a wheelchair and get around. His family created a website for him that I still visit to this day to get updates on his progress: www.CarlRiccioTrust.com.

I don't think I could handle an injury like that; I don't think a lot of people could, honestly. Carl is simply an unbelievable kid, and I could not be more proud of him. His accident was a major family tragedy, but he sets an example for us all.

Angela poses with Rupert Grint, who stars as Ron Weasley in "Harry potter and the Chamber of Secrets."

Hogwarts, flying cars and fun

ANGELA RICCIO

ACCESS ANGELA

THE HOLLYWOOD premiere of "Harry Potter And the Chamber of Secrets" was almost as much fun as the movie. Props and posters were all over, including a flying car and Hogwarts banners that were used in the film. Kids in attendance raced down the red carpet with brooms and wands, dressed up like characters from the movie.

And, of course, it just wouldn't be a red-carpet premiere without all the Hollywood stars dressed up and ready to see the sequel to "Harry Potter."

Joining in on the Harry Potter phenomenon was John Ritter. John told me about his new series called "8 Simple Rules for Dating My Teenage Daughter" on ABC. He told me he was brought to the premiere by his Harry Potter-crazed kids, who really wanted to see the movie.

"Malcolm in the Middle's" Erik Per Sullivan is a Harry Potter fan and also knows what it's like to be young and famous. He told me about how he got his job on "Malcolm."

"It was lots of fun, I basically just had a manager, who sent me to the audition," he said. "The only thing you can do is try your best, and

luckily enough I got the part."

I asked Brian Dunkleman, former host of "American Idol," to really dish the dirt about the show. "You want some dirt," he said jokingly. "Simon's really a woman!"

The highlight of the evening for me was meeting the child stars from "Chamber of Secrets." Emma Watson, 12, who plays Hermionie Grainger, told me she loved this sequel much more than the original.

"I also enjoyed watching it a lot more," she said. "I think 'Chamber of Secrets' is a much better movie; it's funnier and scarier. Just much more fun!"

Next, I met my personal favorite, Rupert Grint, 14, who

plays Ron Weasley. Rupert also preferred this sequel over the original.

"I think definitely 'Chamber of Secrets' is more fun, 'cause I got to do a lot more cool stuff like coughing up slugs and driving a flying car." He said working with Daniel Radcliffe and Emma Watson is the best part of the whole experience. "They're really nice people, and I got to know them better as we filmed the sequel. We work together really well."

I am one of many who hope they continue working together on more "Harry Potter" films for a long time to come.

The only star missing from the event was Harry Potter himself. Unfortunately, Daniel Radcliffe, 13, could not make it to this premiere. But the movie, as I mentioned before, was filled with excitement and adventure. I loved it.

In the words of the late Richard Harris (Dumbledore), "'The Chamber of Secrets' has indeed been opened." So go see it while you still can!

Thirteen-year-old Angela Riccio's column will appear regularly in the teen section. Write to her via e-mail at uteens@presstelegram.com

Angela fulfills her dream to meet the cast of *Harry Potter*. This is my daughter's first column she wrote for *The Long Beach Press Telegram* when she was 13 years old back in 2002.

Irene and I spent New Year's Eve 1993 with Jay Leno at the *Tonight Show* in Los Angeles.

Family portrait from Christmas 2005. Irene, me, Angela and Clairissa with our two dogs, GiGi and Buddy.

My family and I on a trip to New York after we were all finally reunited in 1998.

Irene and I on one of our first dates back in 1985.

Angela interviews rap star Nelly for the syndicated TV show *Extra* in 2005.

My daughter Angela became the 1st writer to win the prestigious "Young Artist Award" for her talent as a teen entertainment journalist.

O.J. signs a football jersey at the Necro Comic Con that we promoted in 2005.

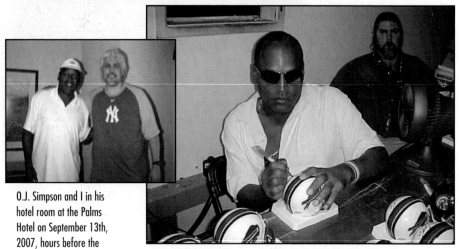

O.J. Simpson and I in his hotel room at the Palms Hotel on September 13th, 2007, hours before the incident in Las Vegas.
Photograph by Lowell Katz.

O.J. Simpson signs NFL memorabilia at the Los Angeles Necro Comic Con. This was the first time O.J. and I had officially worked together.

My two daughters Clairissa and Angela with their puppy C.J., taken Christmas 2007.

Me with Jerry Maren who played "The Lollipop Kid" in the classic film, *The Wizard of Oz*. Jerry signed cards for my *Wizard of Oz* card series.

Irene and I at a recent Yankee's game.

Concept Artist: Jay Lynch

Jay Lynch

©2001 Silly Productions, Inc.

All names and characters used in Silly Cds are strictly fictitious. All cast and images are not based on any actual facts, known or unknown. Some humor may be inappropriate for children under the age of 13.

Final Painting Artist: Tom Bunk

Tom Bunk

If you look closely at the character driving the car in this art, you'll notice that it's actually me!
I'm really honored that I'm forever enshrined in this Silly CD parody of the Beatles.

ANGEL PREMIUM

My daughter Clairissa in 2007, at age 16, in her first month of modeling. She beat out 300 other top models to become "The Angel Jeans Girl" in a worldwide campaign.

Chapter Twenty

THE LUCKIEST HOUSE
2005

I was doing some deals with a business associate named Mark Okin a few years ago. Mark was friends with Frank Robinson, a Hall of Fame baseball player who hit almost 600 home runs and was then the manager of the Montreal Expos. Frank was also a very well respected Major League Baseball executive who spent many years in the Baltimore Orioles organization. One day Frank was in town having lunch with Mark, and my friend asked if I wanted to join them. I wasn't going to miss this opportunity.

I just finished reading an amazing story about Cal Ripken and actor Kevin Costner that supposedly occurred when Ripken, the star shortstop of the Baltimore Orioles, was right in the middle of a consecutive game streak. Ripken had been friends for a long time with Costner who was staying at his house after wrapping up a movie shoot. Ripken was out of the house but came home unexpectedly and found Costner in bed with his wife. Ripken allegedly went crazy, beat up the actor, and was so upset he had to be sedated by a doctor. There was no way he'd be able to play that night. The owner didn't want to interrupt his highly publicized consecutive game streak, which was great for the whole game of baseball, so he shut down some of the light towers at the stadium and blamed it on a power outage. The game had to be cancelled, play resumed the next day, and Ripken showed up to continue his streak.

A power outage had actually occurred at Camden Yards in Baltimore that evening, and the rumor that someone had caused it due to the Costner/Ripken affair

swept the baseball world and continued to circulate despite
many denials from all concerned. It is also a fact that Costner
called in during a local radio talk show to angrily deny the
rumor when the host picked up on the story.

I asked Frank Robinson during lunch if he knew the
truth about this amazing story. "Of course not, Ripken was
actually there at the game that night, suited up, ready to
play before the power outage. It's been well documented.
There are even photos of him in the dugout that night, but
because of the power outage some conspiracy-minded fan
started this story, and it's been around ever since. But it's not
true, not at all. It's bullshit. However, there is something to
the Michael Jordan gambling story that I know is more than
a rumor."

"Everyone knows that Michael Jordan has a big
gambling problem," Robinson said. "A few years ago, Jordan
was playing golf and gambling on each hole with a bunch of
underworld characters. Things went bad when Jordan
refused to pay up his gambling debt, and when the
Commissioner of Basketball was informed of the problem
Jordan had with the mob, he had to deal with it. Jordan was
on the verge of being publicly suspended from playing
basketball, but he was basketball's number one attraction,
and if the news of this story were made public, this gambling
scandal would surely affect attendance at the gates. His
representatives did some heavy negotiating and got him a
deal where he was suspended but not publicly. He was
allowed to 'quit' basketball for a year under the ruse of his
desire to play minor league baseball. The owners of his team,
the Chicago Bulls, also owned a baseball team, the Chicago
White Sox, and they let Jordan stay in shape by playing
baseball on their minor league team while he 'unofficially'
served out his secret suspension in the NBA. When his
suspension for gambling was over, Jordan quit baseball, and
returned to the Bulls just in time for their playoff run as
agreed, and the public never knew the REAL reason why."

It's kind of funny. I just wanted to know some inside
information on the strange Ripken/Costner story, and Frank
Robinson ends up confirming an even stranger story about
Jordan. It was a very interesting afternoon with Frank

Robinson who was also nice enough to sign a few baseballs for me. I was more than happy to pick up the lunch tab.

As I was leaving that lunch with Frank Robinson, I began to think about starting my own memorabilia auction house. I was dealing with all kinds of auction houses at that time by sending my items to be sold off in places like R & R Auctions and a place in Las Vegas called American Memorabilia.

American Memorabilia is owned by a couple of real characters: Kieta and Vic Moreno. A lot of people in the hobby love to tell stories about how Vic was an old hippy drug addict and Kieta was a washed-up stripper, but I truly liked them. They are true inspirations for all of the ex-drug dealers and crack whores of the world because if they could pull their asses up out of the gutter to create a multi-million dollar auction house, then so could I.

The other place I used to turn my memorabilia into cash was a local auction house called Odyssey Auctions in Corona, California. I noticed a young man named Jeff Woolf was the employee who seemed to be doing all the work every time I was there. Eventually I learned he was basically in charge of the whole auction house, which was a very impressive feat at his age. He wrote the catalog copy, made descriptions for the thousands of items in the auction, dealt with the pictures, and was even a respected autograph authenticator. You name it, he did it!

One day when I was at Odyssey to drop off some items for their next auction, Jeff told me that when he was a kid his dad used to go to the police station in Hollywood a few times a week and ask where the big films were being shot on location. The police information officer would tell the general public where the film permits had been issued (this was back before celebrity stalking laws and 9/11). The officer would say something like the Robert DeNiro movie is shooting at such-and-such address in Culver City. His dad would take Jeff along to the set, Jeff would get autographs from all the stars, and his dad would then sell them to Odyssey. When Jeff got older, he got a job at Odyssey and eventually wound up running the place.

I was very impressed with the way Jeff seemed to thrive with all the pressures of running an auction house at such a young age. Dealing with all demanding consignors and buyers was at times very difficult, but he always seemed to take it in good stride. I admired his work ethic. When the owner of Odyssey sold his company to a bigger company called Heritage Auctions, the Heritage people offered Jeff a great job in Dallas, Texas, but he and his wife just bought a house and didn't want to move out of California. Jeff called me and asked, "You want to start our own auction house?" I was in.

We started Universal Rarities Auction House in January 2005. Jeff and I were a good match as partners: He was kind of conservative and knew all the ins and outs of putting together the auction catalog and running the office. I'm a lot more impulsive, and my field of expertise was recruiting consignors to put awesome items in our auctions and buying collections to sell for big profits. We each had different personalities and skills, but together we had everything we needed to run a great business.

However, one of the first big deals we came across at Universal Rarities nearly drove us both to quit. It was the Elvis Audubon Drive Home, also known as the Luckiest House in the World.

In the mid-1950s Elvis Presley bought a house for him and his parents with his first big paycheck. Located at 1034 Audubon Drive in suburban Memphis, it's a big beautiful house in a lovely neighborhood on an acre of land. Unfortunately, it was in a family neighborhood, and anyone could walk right up to the door. Kids used to bang on Elvis's bedroom window in the middle of the night and girls would camp out in the yard. He had no privacy whatsoever. He needed a secluded house with security, looked around, and found his true home: Graceland.

Elvis and the woman who owned Graceland at the time made a deal in which they would swap properties, and Elvis would pay her an additional $50,000 in cash. I owned both original sales agreements signed by Elvis, and they were quite valuable. I had paid $19,000 for the pair of documents at an auction house called Mastronet and wound up selling them separately for a total of more than $100,000.

A year or so after I sold the documents, a woman named Cindy called me out of the blue and said, "I heard you're selling the original contract for the Elvis Presley house on Audubon Drive. We live in that house now."

"Well, I already sold them," I told her, "but I do have a photo copy that I'd be happy to send you."

The lady seemed very excited, "Oh, thanks! That's exactly what we were looking for, because we couldn't afford to buy the original signed documents anyway. We have no money."

We knew all about the house she lived in: The Audubon Drive house was the luckiest house in the world. Everyone who lived there had the most amazing good fortune. The people who sold the house to Elvis were in the oil business. They were completely tapped out and bought the house with their last chunk of money so they'd at least have a place to live. Soon after they moved in, they struck oil and were instantly rich just like *The Beverly Hillbillies*. When they upgraded their house, Elvis bought it for his mother.

Elvis was just at the beginning of his meteoric rise when he bought the place and sunk every dollar he had into this house. Shortly after he and his parents moved in, everything took off for him. He wrote and recorded his first number one song in that house and was offered his first movie contract while he lived there. Elvis hit stardom, and by that time he could afford a showplace like Graceland.

The owner who swapped houses had just gotten her real estate license. The transaction with Elvis was one of her very first deals. She decided to invest in real estate. Even though swapping Graceland for a suburban house did not appear to be a good deal at first glance, once she moved into the house her business took off. She made more than $4 million over the next few years in the real estate business— that was huge money in the 50s. She wound up selling out to a young family whose father had a struggling grocery store.

After he moved into the lucky home on Audubon Drive, his grocery store turned into a chain of very successful small convenience stores and earned him more money than he could spend in two lifetimes. The luck seemed to run out when the convenience store family finally sold the property in 1998. A couple, Cindy and Mike, bought the house thinking they could organize tours of the place for Elvis fans. The neighbors threw a fit, and the town wouldn't grant them the necessary permits. The people at Graceland also did everything they could to stop them. This couple ran into roadblock after roadblock.

Cindy lost her job because the airline she worked at went bankrupt. Mike lost his job at a car lot. It was a terrible run of bad luck. To make ends meet, they gave private illegal tours of the house and let fans sleep there for $100 a night. However, their efforts were not enough. The bank was about to foreclose.

They had bought the house for $180,000 in 1998. It was now 2005, and the house had been officially appraised at $200,000. The house had appreciated $20,000 within 8 years, but it had been on the market for 6 months with no takers.

"We thought this property would be much more valuable," she told me. "We have tons of pictures of Elvis living here, and the house is still decorated almost the same way, because the people who had it before us kept it that way...but still, it's only worth $200,000. We owe $210,000 on it because of a second mortgage, and we have $60,000 in credit card bills. So we need to sell this house for $270,000 just to break even." This was a very compelling story to me.

Cindy negotiated, "Are you interested? We'll sell it to you for $300,000 right now; $30,000 down is all it would take."

This still seemed like a great offer. The real estate market had gone through the roof just about everywhere in America except the South. In Los Angeles, houses like that famous Elvis place would go for over a million dollars no matter who owned the house. Maybe someone would think it's a bargain at five times its value because of the historical significance.

My wife, a big Elvis fan who would have been happy to get out of L.A. for a while, was all for the idea and suggested that I take it, but eventually I decided it would be too much of a hassle. I didn't know anyone in Memphis who could keep an eye on the property until I resold it.

I called a guy who deals in real estate all over the world, and he said, "Other than Graceland, I wouldn't touch a house in Memphis. No one wants to live there." Boy, was he wrong. Once again I should've gone with my first instinct and purchased the place for 30 grand down, but I let myself get talked out of it and went with plan B.

"You have another option," I told Cindy when I called her back. "Put the house in my auction. I know I could get you $300,000." We talked for a bit, and she went to talk it over with her husband.

She wasn't sure when she called me back. "If we put the house in your auction catalog, it will take three months to sell, and we don't have three months. We can't pay the mortgage; the bank is about to foreclose. We don't have enough money to live here for three months."

"I will give you $2,000 right now," I told her. "If the house doesn't sell at my auction, you keep the money."

You would have thought I was sending them a fortune. This couple got so excited. "Send us the $2,000! Wire it to us right away! When do we get it? We need the money yesterday!"

My partner and I decided to set the reserve price for the house at $300,000. That meant if no one was willing to pay that amount, the auction was off and they'd get to keep our $2,000. We sent our standard agreement for them to sign, and Cindy called me back.

"You get 15 percent in this agreement; our real estate agent is only getting 3 percent. Why do you get 15?"

"The bottom line is that you are gonna clear $300,000, and your real estate agent has had this house listed for months; she's not going to sell it. I will."

"Well, we need more money then. Make the reserve $400,000."

"All right, fine," I figured the house would bring in a lot more. My partner was very annoyed. "It's never going to stop now," he warned me. "Once they start with the demands, it only gets worse."

"It'll be fine. I think we can get a million dollars for this house!" I had a vision and didn't want to listen to what my partner was saying. I knew this could be a huge auction and wanted the business badly. I was going to market it to Elvis fans worldwide, not only as the Elvis house, but also as the Luckiest House in the World.

I sent out a new contract with a new reserve price of $400,000. Soon enough I got a phone call from Cindy. "We want more money. We can't wait three months for this sale to happen, we'll need at least $5,000 cash to keep going."

That was it for my partner. "Screw them!" he said emphatically. "Forget this whole thing." But I wasn't willing to let it go. I got her down to $3,500 and agreed to send them the money out of my own pocket.

The husband Mike who I hadn't dealt with much got on the phone and was very grateful. "It's a done deal Tom! Thanks! Now send the money, send the money!"

"Fine, but we need you to sign the contract first." All of a sudden, Cindy got back on the phone.

"Now wait a minute here. We had our real estate agent go over this contract, and she told us it says you're getting a 20 percent buyers' commission in this deal on top of the 15 percent. You're getting a 35 percent commission?"

"Yes, but that doesn't matter to you," I explained. "The buyer's fee does not come out of your money. You will get your $400,000 if it sells."

"So the buyer has to pay you an extra 20 percent, and you're getting 15 percent from us?" she demanded. "Forget it, we're not signing anything where you get 35 percent!"

"Listen, your real estate agent is getting three percent of nothing.... I'm going to make this happen for you. Cindy, I promise you I will get this done."

"Forget it!" She hung up. Soon enough she called back and demanded, "We want $500,000 guaranteed."

I could not believe this and pointed out, "$400,000 is just the reserve. You may get more than that. Besides, you are losing your house."

She ignored that. "And we need the auction to happen within 30 days, and we need $5,000 right now."

My partner was pissed, "We are not giving them any money, you are not going out there, and we are not doing this. Please, let's forget this deal now!"

But I could not let this go. The real problem was that they wouldn't or couldn't wait three months for the auction to happen; their financial situation was that bad. I decided to offer to have a Universal Rarities auction on eBay. I called

Mike back and outlined this idea for him. Mike had been great, but his wife was the one who was completely out of control.

"We just don't have the money Tom. We can't afford to wait," Mike said apologetically.

"Well, let's put it on eBay. I've sold Elvis's hair on eBay. I have a bunch of big Elvis fans in England to reach out to. So let's do it right away."

"You can do an auction of a house on eBay?" he asked, completely amazed.

"Sure, yes, I can have it done and over within 30 days. So let's get the consignment agreement signed right now!"

He put the phone down for a few minutes and went to talk to his wife. He came back and said, "I'm really sorry Tom. Cindy doesn't like the vibe. She thinks you're being too greedy."

"I'm being greedy? You've got to be kidding me!" I think if you look up the word "greedy" in the dictionary, you'll see Cindy's picture there.

The bottom line is they took all of my ideas and got a friend of theirs to put the house up for sale on eBay. Even Nicolas Cage, a huge Elvis fan, saw all the uproar and made inquiries but was not the high bidder. The house wound up selling for $910,000. Every selling point I'd mentioned was right there in bullet points on eBay. The biggest piece of Elvis memorabilia in the world! Elvis's first home! The luckiest house in the world! I couldn't believe my eyes; I was beyond pissed.

Here's another amazing act of greed by her: One of the under bidders contacted them directly after the auction and offered them $1.2 million for the house, so she reneged on the original eBay sale. I called Mike up after the sale, and Cindy answered the phone.

The bitch said, "Oh Tom, we would have liked to go with you for this, but you just wanted too much. We gave our friend three percent to put the house on eBay, and he was happy with that. We're celebrating with him right now."

"Anyway Cindy, I called to talk to Mike, but I'm gonna tell you what you did was screwed up."

"You made your own bed...you were too greedy."
Then she went off to celebrate. The last I heard was that the
original winner of the house on eBay was suing Cindy over
the deal and all the parties were involved in a huge lawsuit.
The whole thing made me sick to my stomach, and my
partner said, "Tom, I don't ever want to hear about Mike and
Cindy or this house ever again."

I went home that night trying to put the matter
behind me and vented one last time to my wife about what a
witch Cindy was. When I was done she turned to me and
said, "Well, they're leaving that place millionaires, just like
everybody else. I guess that house was lucky for them after
all."

Here's the kicker: Mike returned my call a few weeks
later to thank me and apologize for how the whole matter
had turned out. Mike seemed happy and upbeat; he told me
that he and Cindy were divorcing.

"Oh, I'm sorry to hear that," I said, a little taken
aback.

"No, no," he said with feeling. "It's a good thing,
believe me."

The financial freedom Mike received by selling his
share of the house made it possible for him to divorce Cindy,
and that may have made him the luckiest guy who ever
owned that house.

The sale of the house made worldwide news and the
whole thing was my idea, but somehow in the end I was cut
out. My auction house got no publicity, and I never received
a dime from the sale for my time.

Chapter Twenty-One

HOLLYWOOD HILLS/
ANNA NICOLE SMITH
2007

Dave, another friend of mine in the business, owns an autograph shop in Hollywood. A few years ago he called to tell me he had a bunch of Anna Nicole Smith memorabilia: old cancelled checks, two of her diaries, an old driver's license, and stuff like that. Apparently, when Anna left town, a bunch of her old crap was tossed in the garbage. Someone thought the junk might have some value, retrieved it from her trash can, and sold her discarded stuff to him for practically nothing. This was about the time her show on the E! Channel was ending, and all I could think was, "Who cares?" It seemed like she had already peaked in terms of her fame. Dave would have let all this stuff go for a few hundred dollars, but I wasn't interested. Neither was anybody else at the time.

I will admit the diary was pretty entertaining if only in terms of shock value. She wrote openly about her sex life including being screwed with a Coke bottle by an angry lover and forcing another guy who had cheated on her to stick his tongue up her ass for hours at a time. Raunchy and shamelessly funny? Yes. Valuable? I didn't think so at that time.

A couple years later Anna was all over the news when she gave birth to a new baby girl, and a few days later her 20-year-old son Daniel died suddenly and mysteriously in the Bahamas. Interest in Anna exploded on worldwide headline news. I thought, "It might be kind of interesting to have these diaries."

I called Dave and he said, "Believe me, I'm thinking the same thing you are. The problem is I can't find them anymore. I never sold them, but I don't know where I put them. I'll let you know if I find them."

A few more months passed, and then Anna Nicole passed away herself under mysterious circumstances. I saw Dave at an autograph show and he said, "Tom, I found the diaries!" He was trying to make a deal for $100,000 with another company, but it fell through. We worked out our own deal for everything, which included two diaries, all the checks, and I.D. cards for $50,000.

Dave was okay with providing me a $5,000 commission if I found an investor for the deal. I advised my investor that it was a good deal and was completely upfront about the kickback. He agreed it was a good deal. After he financed the deal for $50,000, I would sell everything and split the profits with him. This was one of those no-brainer deals that only come around once in a while. The key to this deal wasn't just about the value of the items; it was also about the value of the information inside the diaries.

A few months earlier Dave couldn't sell that Anna shit for a roll of dimes. Then the whole world suddenly wanted to know EVERYTHING about Anna, and these diaries provided her innermost thoughts. Not exactly the thoughts of Einstein I realized—story after story she wrote of her crazy sexcapades—but hell, I'm all for giving the people what they want.

We hired my partner's dad Steve Woolf to gauge the interest for the information in the diaries; he wound up talking to *People* magazine who referred us to the *Splash News* agency and Phoenix Books, a book publisher who was doing a tell-all book about Anna Nicole by her half-sister entitled *Train Wreck*. By the end of the day, the deals we made with *Splash* and Phoenix got my investors $50,000 back! We'd already broken even and hadn't even sold a thing, just the rights to reproduce a few pages from the diaries. We had plenty more of where that came from!

*   *   *

Every media outlet in town wanted me to come on their shows to speak about the Anna memoirs and the upcoming sale of the diaries in our auction, but no one wanted to pay me. Every show producer said, "Come on Tom, we'll promote the sale of the diaries in your auction, and you'll get more customers if you come on the show, but we can't pay you anything." I wanted to figure out a way to capitalize more off this opportunity. Then it hit me! I could get a sponsor to pay me for each show I mentioned their name on.

The first sponsor I thought of was GoldenPalace.com, an online gambling site that had difficulty finding places where they were allowed to advertise. This sponsor was willing to pay for unusual advertising opportunities. I've seen them advertise in all kinds of weird ways including paying a guy to tattoo their name on his forehead. I contacted them though a company called Advertag, and we immediately struck a deal. I would get paid $5,000 for each show I went on and mentioned that GoldenPalace.com was sponsoring the Anna Nicole Diaries.

After a few shows, I asked for my money. "Oh, it's coming Tom. Just keep up the good work, your check is on the way," they replied. I'd do several more shows and still no money. "Don't worry Tom. Golden Palace is a big company. We'll pay you."

They wanted to keep it going so they wired me $12,000, and I continued to promote them on tons of shows that aired worldwide, but I pulled the plug when their bill exceeded $50,000. "Where's the rest of my money?" I wanted to know.

"Some of the shows you did never aired in some countries we wanted to reach," my contact said.

"I'm not the fucking program director to the world," I explained. "I can't tell them what countries to air my segments in."

"Well, we aren't paying you the rest of the money we owe you," said the prick.

I have a lawyer trying to serve a complaint on them, but as unbelievable as it seems, no one in the world knows where the offices of GoldenPalace.com is located. I've got to hand it to them—they've got me for now.

We went on to make big deals with a lot of publications including *US* and *In Touch* magazines. I thought we had a time frame of two or three days before the interest faded away, but the death of Anna Nicole was probably the biggest story of 2007. I was still getting besieged with media requests on the whole Anna Diaries thing and knew I needed another sponsor to keep this going strong.

My auction house partner Jeff and I are both fans of *The Howard Stern Radio Show*. Jeff suggested we contact their sponsor Clips4sale.com, a porn site that had a hard time advertising because of their triple X adult content. We immediately did a deal with them and went back on all the TV shows to promote the upcoming Anna Diary Auction and Clips4sale.com.

The story kept going, and I was getting booked everywhere: *Geraldo Rivera, Entertainment Tonight, Access Hollywood, Nancy Grace,* CNN, Court TV.... I was so happy that my sponsor was advertised everywhere from magazines to TV to TMZ.com, who actually placed a link to the Clips4sale.com website for viewing real pages of the Anna Nicole Diaries. While I was on the shows, I told people, "We can't talk about everything in the diaries. There's much more. If you want to actually read the diaries, go to Clips...The number 4...Sale...Dot...Com." That was a huge deal, and the best part was that they paid us on time, every time. Our arrangement worked out well for everyone. Things were plugging away, and the fascination over Anna Nicole seemed like it would never end.

In the middle of the craze, a guy named Eric Redding called me to say he was once Anna's agent and had written a book about his experiences with her. He saw the money we got for her diaries and wanted to know if I wanted to represent the three Anna Nicole diaries he had. I asked him how he got them, and he claimed he was Anna's friend and she had given them to him. Eric wanted a $100,000 reserve for all 3 of the diaries. He e-mailed me a few random pages from the diaries, and I had them authenticated. They were the real deal. I read a page where Anna was mad at Eric for inappropriately touching her and asked him about it. He said that he had decided not to sell that diary but wanted $200,000 for the other two.

I had flash backs of Cindy and the rising reserve on her Elvis house. I told Eric I was no longer interested, and he said that was fine because the diaries actually belonged to Anna's ex-boyfriend. He was also afraid that the FBI would take the diaries away from him. I was feeling more concerned by the minute and was happy to dodge a bullet with this guy.

A week later, Geraldo asked me to talk about the successful sale of our Anna Nicole diaries on his show. Then he casually mentioned he was having author Eric Redding on the same show to promote his book about Anna. I told Geraldo what I knew about Eric. He said, "Even better, we'll confront him about his stolen diaries. It'll be fun."

Geraldo was right. Eric came on via satellite from somewhere in Texas, and I was surprised to see him for the first time; He looked exactly like the little actor David Spade—if Spade were on crack! Geraldo let Eric talk about his book for a while. When he asked about the diaries, Eric started to shit his pants. Then Geraldo cut to me with all of Eric's printed e-mails where he talks of his fear of the FBI and all the crap that Anna wrote about this weasel in her diaries. It was pretty funny watching him run off the set between segments. It was classic Geraldo!

Things kept getting better. Our auction house Universal Rarities broke records with the Anna Nicole Smith Diaries Auction. Her memoirs sold for more than any other diaries in history. However, out of the blue, the Virginia Tech Mass Murder tragedy struck, and all of a sudden I was yesterday's news. The phones stopped ringing, and all my appearances got cancelled. Instead of me calling up and saying, "Okay, I could do your show next Thursday," I was begging, "Will you please let me on your show?"

I received responses like, "We have other things to talk about, Anna Nicole's dead. It's over." Boy, did it suck to see that gravy train ride out of my life, but as it always seems to happen just as one gravy train leaves, another one comes around the corner.

Soon after news of our record-breaking Anna Nicole diary sale hit the wire, all kinds of people called us wanting to cash in on the recent Anna Nicole craze: "Hi, I'm Anna's old friend. I have lots of her dirty underwear and a needle we used to share drugs. Are you interested in placing them in your next auction?" or "Hi, I'm one of Anna's lesbian lovers. I have lots of butt-plugs and dildo's we used on each other. Can you sell them for me?"

The strangest thing occurred when we got a call from a doctor's wife in Texas who sent us a tape of Anna Nicole Smith undergoing breast enhancement surgery. She was lying there on the operating table unconscious and nude with a bunch of tattoos all over, and I do mean all over: weird tattoos like a sleeping Mexican guy in a sombrero and a Bugs Bunny tattoo located right above her bush. I don't get it.

I like naked woman as much as anyone, but I don't understand how anyone could get a kick out of watching a doctor rip open a woman and shove balloons in her chest. It's not exactly what I'd call entertainment.

The doctor who performed the surgery on Anna was now retired and seemed to be a bit out of it. It was obvious that his wife was the one running the show. She claimed that Anna Nicole's death voided any patient confidentiality laws, and after she saw me auctioning off the diaries, she wanted me to sell her Anna Nicole Breast Surgery Tape.

I had the tape and thought I'd see if there was any interest. I wasn't optimistic, but I called some people at a couple of shows, and they were all very anxious to see the tape. Plenty of people wanted it badly including mainstream outlets like *Entertainment Tonight*. Since Carnie Wilson's live tape of her gastric bypass surgery made three quarters of a million dollars, I shouldn't have been surprised.

As amazing as it sounds, my friend Dave who sold me the Anna Nicole diaries lived right next door to Anna Nicole's Los Angeles home. Since Larry Birkhead, the biological father of Anna's baby daughter, inherited Anna's home, I thought I'd go over with my wife to meet him.

When we walked by the house, the front door was wide open and we heard a baby crying. A maid came out with her arms full of boxes and walked down the street toward the dumpster with the front door still wide open. Irene and I looked at each other and couldn't believe it. Anyone could have walked right in and snatched baby Dannielynn! When the maid returned, we introduced ourselves and left her my phone number for Birkhead who wasn't home at the time.

The next day Birkhead called, and after I told him that I was the guy who auctioned the Anna Diaries, he wanted to get together at a nearby country club. Irene and I got there on time, but Birkhead was late. After about 10 minutes, I got a call, "Hi, it's me, Larry. I'm on my way into the restaurant."

I looked outside and saw a large man with a small woman walking towards the restaurant. When they got closer, I realized it was actually Larry Birkhead and his large woman companion. It was the strangest thing to meet him in person after I'd seen him on TV a thousand times. He is literally this small, 98-pound weakling with long stringy hair and a baseball cap; he looks like a teenager even though he's got to be pushing 40.

Some public opinion was against Birkhead for selling pictures of his famous baby daughter to the press, but I had no problem with it. Larry was actually a paparazzi photographer before he met Anna Nicole. All the people at *Splash* and the other big photo agencies remember him well. He was out peddling pictures of Jennifer Lopez and anyone else to get some lunch money. His life and fortune changed when he was taking pictures of Anna Nicole and she leaned over and said, "Hey, you're cute!"

Encouraged, Larry approached her as she sat at her table with a bunch of people and said, "I'd love to do a private shoot with you."

She reciprocated his interest on the spot. "Here's my number, call me anytime." (This original meeting was captured on tape. I saw it on a Hollywood biography story of Anna Nicole on TV.) At the time they met, Anna Nicole wanted another baby and was looking for a father with blue eyes, fair hair, and clear skin. Apparently, Larry fit the bill.

Larry and his female companion joined us at the table. He knew about me and my company from all the publicity I've received from our recent Anna Nicole Auction. We chatted about that for a minute or two. He mentioned that he had recently lost 30 pounds, and my wife jokingly asked, "What's your secret?"

"Oh, you wouldn't want to do it this way—the stress diet," he told her seriously. "I've had a hard time eating and sleeping."

Now that Larry is the one in the spotlight, hoards of paparazzi are following him around, chasing him down, invading his privacy, and making his life as miserable as he has done to others in the past. Even with all the money and fame he's inherited along with his baby, he'd probably prefer to go back to his simple life. My wife and I felt sorry for him.

I had a couple of reasons to meet with Larry Birkhead, and it was time to get down to the business at hand: "I have a copy of one of the diaries we sold in our auction where Anna Nicole professes her love for her husband Howard Marshall. This diary is all about how much she adores him and wants to take care of him and so on. You may need this in court one day."

Everyone knows that Howard Marshall was Anna Nicole Smith's 90-year-old billionaire husband who died while he was married to Anna and left his fortune to be disputed between Anna and Marshall's family. Since Dannielynn is the only living heir to Anna Nicole's estate, she just might be the one who inherits the Marshall family fortune.

The Marshall family had claimed that Anna Nicole was just a gold digger who didn't love Howard Marshall, and therefore was not entitled to any claim on the estate. However, the copy of the diary, written in Anna's own hand, shows her professing her undying love for her elderly and sick husband.

Larry was so soft-spoken it was hard to hear him. "That's what you wanted to tell me? This could help, I appreciate it."

"One other thing…that tape of Anna Nicole having surgery, I have it. I'm hoping you'll endorse it. I'll give Dannielynn a cut out of my share, and it will be better received by everyone."

Larry looked skeptical. "Are you sure that's really her?"

"Oh yes, I'm really sure." I pulled out a portable DVD player and showed him the tape right there.

"I guess she had some of those tattoos removed at some point," Larry said when it was over. "This is just too personal and private. For me, this is not a marketable tape; I can't endorse it." I understood his decision.

"There is something," Larry said, "I have storage sheds just packed with her things...checks, clothes, accessories...stuff the baby will never have any use for. I'd like to turn it all into money for her future. I should probably liquidate it all now."

The kind of stuff that normal people would just get rid of in a garage sale had lots of value to Anna fans. "Absolutely, I can help you there," I told him. "Let's do a big Universal Rarities Anna Nicole Smith Estate Auction!"

"Great, let me talk to Howard and firm up the details," Birkhead said. Howard K. Stern was Anna Nicole's longtime lawyer and companion. He handled all of Anna's affairs and was appointed as executor of the Anna Nicole Smith estate.

Next thing I knew my phone was ringing, and I had a furious lawyer on the line. It was Howard K. Stern saying, "I saw what you did with the diaries. Those were stolen! Now you have videotapes of Anna's surgery out there! This is the tackiest sleaziest thing! We're going to sue you and your company and...."

"Hold on a minute there Howard," I said. "Listen to me. First of all the diaries we represented were in no way stolen, and as for the tape, I realize that this is a personal matter to you given your relationship with Anna Nicole, and I get that, but try to understand that this is just business for me," I explained.

Stern calmed down long enough to ask me some questions. "Who owns those tapes?" he asked.

"They belong to a consigner who is the wife of the doctor who performed the surgery in the video," I answered.

"Well that's illegal. I'm going to sue you and them unless I get this tape," he stated.

"I can't give you this tape Howard because it is not mine. I swear it is just a consignment from a couple in Texas. I am not allowed to give you this tape Howard. In fact I've made up my mind that I don't need all this hassle. I really don't want a fight with you or the consignors, so I'm just sending the tape back to Texas, and you can fight directly with them."

The whole thing became a tug of war between lawyers for the consignor in Texas and Howard K. Stern. Howard was quick to act with a restraining order for the tape. Somehow he got the court in Los Angeles to order us to turn the tape over to Howard until a judgment could be made. The lawyers in Texas were pissed.

"Just send me the tape now," the Texan lawyer said. "You can say that you didn't get the restraining order until after you sent me the tapes."

"No way in hell! There's no way I'm going to jail so that some lady can get her stupid videotape back by violating a court order!"

I complied with the court order. Larry called to thank me and asked me to call Howard back about following through with the Anna Nicole Estate Auction.

Howard was in a much calmer mood as he reflected on his relationship with Anna Nicole. "I really loved her," Howard declared, "and I only want what's best for Dannielynn. There's no way in the world I would ever profit off a tape like that Tom, and if you would commit to never again represent that tape or any other sleazy tapes of Anna that may pop up, I will submit a settlement agreement in writing excluding you from the lawsuit I am filing against those people in Texas, and I'll also forgive you for dealing in all those other personal diaries and stuff that belonged to Anna."

I knew Howard K. Stern loves to sue people, but I also knew that I'd done nothing wrong. Suing people is a part of business, but I'd rather patch things up with a person and do more business with them. On July 20, 2007, I received a settlement agreement signed by Howard and was hoping we could move forward and work together to liquidate the Anna Nicole estate by turning Anna's useless salt and pepper shakers into cash that her daughter may be able to use somewhere down the road.

I had one more idea. Anna Nicole's house, now Birkhead and Dannielynne's home, was on a cliff way up in the Hollywood Hills. It's a beautiful property but not kid-friendly. If you go to the back of the house, you can see that it drops straight down hundreds of feet. This house is great for adults who don't drink much, but it's certainly not for kids.

I thought maybe I should try again with the house situation. Elvis's house had gotten many times over its market value, and I bet I could do it again with this beautiful Hollywood house. It couldn't be hyped in the same way that Elvis's original home could be, but I figured her fans could enjoy living in the home they'd seen on her reality show. I thought it was worth a shot to see if we can work out a deal to sell the place.

Everyone got on board. Everything was moving ahead great; I was talking to Howard every week or so. I found it very strange that he still had a message from Anna Nicole on his voicemail saying, "Hi, me and Howard are busy right now. Be a dear and leave a message and we'll get right back to you," in a sexy Marilyn Monroe-like whisper. I wondered how long it would be before he changed it, because I found it a bit creepy. In the end, they agreed to do a big auction of Anna's estate crap with us, scheduled for January 2008. We set a big meeting for September 20, 2007, to make the final arrangements and sign the consignment agreement.

Unfortunately, the small matter of O.J. intervened the week before the deal was signed. You can guess what happened with our agreement to represent the Anna Nicole estate in our auction....

Chapter Twenty-Two

O.J. SIMPSON ROUND TWO AUGUST - SEPTEMBER 2007

The year 2007 was quickly becoming our most successful ever. On top of our regular auctions, which were improving with each catalog, the Anna Nicole Diaries Auction broke records, and all the signs were pointing to things getting even better. I was right in the middle of three of the biggest deals of my life. We were finalizing a deal with Steiner Sports to make their vast inventory of more than 15,000 items available for consignment in all our upcoming auctions, the Anna Nicole Estate Auction was becoming a reality, and we were in negotiations with Dallas Gold & Silver to merge with their great auction house. Our future looked bright!

It was mid-August, and I went to the Silver Classic Car Auction in Reno, Nevada, where we warmed up the classic car-buying fans by auctioning off vintage autographed memorabilia onstage each morning before the auction started.

I was coming off stage one morning at the car show when my cell phone rang: "Hi Tom, I saw you on TV with the Anna Nicole diaries. Congratulations," said a somewhat familiar voice.

"Who is this?" I asked.

"Al!"

"Al who?"

"Al Beardsley, you remember me, don't you?" A chill literally ran down my spine. This was one person I had never wanted to hear from again in my life. He was back from the dead and calling me on the phone!

"Uh Al, so what do you want, man?"

"Just calling to congratulate you Tom. Oh and by the way, I wanted to tell you that I have an even bigger and better collection than the one you just sold for hundreds of thousands of dollars."

"Oh yeah, what is it?"

"O.J. Simpson's personal items—all his plaques, a bunch of his awards, record-breaking footballs, personal, unpublished, family photographs. You name it, I've got it."

I should have just hung up the phone, but I had to see where this was going. I knew Beardsley was an O.J. fanatic, but how did he get his hands on a collection like that? I asked him for the details. He told me these were items stolen from O.J.'s house on Rockingham Drive by his former agent Mike Gilbert many years ago, because O.J. refused to pay Mike the money he owed him. Beardsley was very clear that he didn't want O.J. to know about this. He told me he didn't want me to do a public auction; he wanted this to go on the down-low in order to avoid O.J.'s wrath. He asked if I could find a high-end private collector. I told him I'd get back to him.

Beardsley, being Beardsley, called me back several times the next day to bug me about this collection. I couldn't quite figure it out. Is he setting me up, or is he just crazy enough to think that I'd actually be interested in fencing his stolen goods? As soon as I got back to my auction house in Corona, California, I told my partner Jeff about the situation. He said, "You're crazy if you talk to Beardsley, O.J., or anyone else without going to the police to tell them what's going on."

I agreed and immediately called the local police. I was on hold for about two hours while being switched around from department to department. No one wanted to hear about this. "I'm calling about a bunch of O.J. Simpson's stolen stuff." Robbery division didn't want it; burglary division didn't want it. They thought I should call the Brentwood police and switched me back and forth. Finally after asking me a few more questions, someone decided that the whole thing sounded like a civil matter between O.J., his agents, and some autograph dealers. Bottom line: they didn't want to get involved. They thought I was wasting their time, but I was more upset about wasting mine.

I knew O.J. from that autograph signing we did with him in 2005 and felt obligated to inform him of what was going on. "Hi O.J., it's Tom Riccio. I thought you should know that our favorite loony bird Al Beardsley is somehow still alive, and he's been calling me the past few days," I said.

"This can't be good." O.J. guessed correctly.

"Well, Al claims he has all kinds of personal stuff including a lot of your awards, record-breaking footballs, plaques, and your old personal family photographs that were all stolen from your place in Brentwood," I told him.

O.J. went through the roof. "I've been looking for that stuff for years Tom! I know that fucking weasel Mike Gilbert stole the stuff. He must've given it to that nutcase Al to fence. You've got to help me get that stuff back, man. It's all my personal stuff, and this is not about the money. When I die, I want my kids to have these things!"

He filled me in on the background. Apparently, he had employed a guy named Michael Gilbert at one point. Somebody from the Los Angeles Police Department had called the Simpson house in Brentwood to tip O.J. off that the police were about to execute a raid on his property and confiscate everything they could get their hands on. This was in order to settle a judgment Fred Goldman had won against O.J. in the civil suit. This was the raid where they got O.J.'s famous Heisman Trophy and other valuable stuff. The police had a huge inventory list of all the things they were after but didn't get nearly all of it.

O.J. was out of town, but while the police were on the way, Michael Gilbert and O.J.'s sister packed up everything they could get their hands on and put it in their cars. Gilbert was going to hold onto the items just for safekeeping— supposedly he could be trusted. He and O.J. had disputes over fees Gilbert said O.J. owed him, they parted ways, and he started selling things off piece by piece over the next few years. Eventually he ran into some real money trouble and put the rest of the collection up as collateral against a big loan that he never paid back. Somehow Al Beardsley got his hands on the record-breaking game balls, autographed photographs signed to O.J. from people like J. Edgar Hoover, and his Hall of Fame plaque.

I told O.J. that I had called the police, and they basically told me they didn't want to do anything about the theft. O.J. said, "I'm O.J. Simpson, of course the Los Angeles Police aren't gonna help me. Try to get me a list of all the stolen shit he has, then I'll call you back soon, and we'll figure this all out. Don't worry Tom. I'll take care of you for helping me with this. I know I owe you one."

The next day the FBI called to inform me that they wanted to speak to me about an investigation they were doing regarding the doctor's wife who'd tried to sell the Anna Nicole Smith surgery videotape. I told the agents I'd be happy to meet with them, but I also wanted to speak to them about this O.J. Simpson stolen goods situation. They agreed, and I went to meet the FBI agents at the offices of Larry Birkhead's lawyer in downtown Los Angeles.

Beardsley called again. "I'm going to need at least $100,000 dollars for all this stuff Tom. Do you think you can get this done?"

"I don't know Al. Can you send me an inventory list of all the stuff?" I asked.

"I've got a list here for all the items, but the personal photos are somewhere else. A guy I know bought them from a public storage auction after O.J.'s mom refused to pay her bill for the rent on the storage unit. I guess the bitch is a big deadbeat, just like her son." Beardsley rambled.

I told O.J. what Al had said, and he was even more pissed. "You know that whack-job is talking about my dead mother!" I think if Al had been in front of him at that point, O.J. might've committed a double-murder on him alone! "My mother never had any storage shed. It's all a load of bullshit. They stole those family photos along with all my other shit, and we're gonna get it all back!"

I told O.J. that I could tell the FBI about this, and maybe they could figure out a way to recover his stuff, but O.J. wasn't buying it. "Fuck the police! Fuck the FBI! You really think that once they hear the name O.J. Simpson, they're gonna run to help me? Hell no! Here's what I think we should do Tom," he explained. "Let's tell Beardsley that we have a rich buyer who will pay big bucks for all the shit, then we set it all up to happen at your auction house. When Al and his cohorts show up to sell the stuff, I show up to bust them while cameras pop out like *Dateline NBC* and announce, 'It ain't nice to try and squeeze the Juice. You're busted!' That would be priceless TV, Tom. Whatdaya think?"

"Let me get back to you on that O.J." I told him.

I went to speak to my partner Jeff about O.J.'s proposal. He started, "You know I respect your opinions when it comes to business, but are you fucking out of your mind! We're NOT going to host this O.J. Simpson Dog and Pony Show at our place of business. This is where I work five or six days a week. O.J. is not going to turn Universal Rarities into his personal Undercover Sting Operation Office. It's not gonna happen! You're going to see the FBI tomorrow regarding that Anna Nicole videotape, talk to them about this O.J. crap, and see if they can come up with any good ideas because I don't think getting our auction house involved would be good for business."

I never knew how right Jeff would be: O.J. plus public business equals failed business.

I went to the office of Larry Birkhead's lawyer where I was introduced to a female FBI agent from Los Angeles and a male FBI agent from Houston. I told the agents, "Listen, I had kind of an interesting situation pop up, and I want to tell you about it."

"Okay, what have you got?"

I told them the whole story of how Beardsley contacted me about selling O.J.'s stolen goods. They listened to me, asked a few questions, and then went out of the room to confer.

They came back in and one of them said, "Look. This didn't just happen yesterday. This alleged theft occurred many years ago. This guy didn't break into the house himself and steal it. He just claims to have it in his possession. It sounds like a civil matter; I think the local police are right. Be careful, talk to your lawyer about this, call O.J. and see what he wants to do, but there's no reason for us to get involved at this point. Besides we are here to get information from you regarding Anna Nicole Smith, not O.J. Simpson or any other celebrities that you may have had experiences with. So please, let's get back to the issue we came for." That was the end of that with the FBI.

O.J. called back and informed me that his lawyer had put an end to the auction house sting with TV cameras, because a public appearance in California where he was recovering valuable memorabilia would attract the wrath of the Goldmans who would seize all his personal stuff. O.J. told me, "If we do this in California, you know in a blink of an eye we'll get a visit from Fred Goldman a.k.a. Fred Gold-Digger."

A week or so later Al called and said, "Listen, I need to bring this stuff in from out of state."

"Wait a minute, where is it?" I asked.

"Las Vegas," he said.

I talked to O.J. and told him the stuff was actually in Vegas. O.J. said, "I'm coming out to Vegas for a wedding in a couple of weeks. Why don't we just get the stuff while I'm there?"

It turned out that O.J. was going to be in Vegas the same weekend I was flying home from a meeting with Steiner Sports in New York, and I figured I could make a quick stop in Las Vegas before returning home to L.A. Everything just seemed to jive for that weekend.

Beardsley called nearly every day, pressing to get the deal done. I kept telling him to wait until the week of September 10. Beardsley very much wanted to make this happen and agreed to show up in Vegas that week to broker O.J.'s stolen stuff to a wealthy client I told him I had lined up.

Jeff and I met with Pete Kelly of Steiner Sports on Friday, September 7. We made a deal where Universal Rarities Auction House was going to have access to sell the thousands of items in Steiner's inventory in our future auctions. It was a home run!

After the Steiner deal, Jeff went back to California while I stayed a few extra days to visit family in New Jersey and left for Las Vegas on Wednesday, September 12. My friend Lowell booked a room for me at Palace Station, a two-thousand-room hotel preferred by locals that sits about a block off the strip.

O.J. called me the minute I landed and invited me to join his private party at some huge strip club, but I was anxious to talk to him about exactly what we were going to do the following day. We arranged to meet the next day to go over the game plan. Later on, I spoke to Al Beardsley who threatened, "Tom, this better happen, or I'm charging you $500 per day for my time!"

I had taped weird Al in the past, but I didn't have a recorder with me at that time. I went to a Vegas Radio Shack where I was told they were out of the old-fashioned cassette recorders, but the new digital ones were better. They require no tapes and could record up to 144 hours of dialogue. I bought one and went back to my hotel to test it out by placing it on top of the tall TV cabinet. It worked perfectly! If Beardsley were to go off, I knew that my new recorder would document every second of his antics. If he ever denied that he knew exactly where those items were stolen from, I could play that back for O.J. so he would have no doubt that Al is a lying piece of crap.

The next afternoon, I headed over to O.J.'s hotel to go over the details of the bust and to finalize the deal about my compensation in this situation. I recorded our deal just in case someone were to forget the details of our agreement.

O.J. was staying at the Palms, a very happening Vegas hotel that's popular with young celebrities. I wandered through the lobby and found O.J. poolside having a great time. He greeted me with a loud, "Hey Tom! How you doing, buddy?" He was so boisterous it made me nervous. I wanted to keep a low profile.

I wanted a private conversation with O.J. but that was impossible. Hundreds of young gorgeous girls in bikinis were wandering around, drinks were flowing, and O.J. was busy telling stories and cracking jokes. If you just met him and didn't know he was involved in the notorious double murder of his wife and her friend, you would never believe he could do something like that. Anyone would immediately like the guy; he has great charisma.

A few of these pretty girls came up to O.J. and wanted to sit on his lap, take photos, and flirt with him. It was like 1975, and he was at the height of his football fame all over again. I couldn't believe it! I knew he had to be about 60 years old, but he didn't look or act it. Guys were coming over to shake his hand and ask for autographs. Everyone was buying him drinks and inviting him to private cabanas. He was literally shoving girls off his lap. Plenty of people hate O.J. Simpson, but you'd never know it at this public party. He was, by far, the most popular person there. It was unbelievable!

At one point, an older black man approached O.J. who looked to be in his 70s. He didn't look like Yale Galanter, the man everyone always sees on TV as O.J.'s lawyer, but that's how O.J. identified him to me. O.J. told him why I was there, and this man just shook his head. He tried to persuade O.J. not to do anything himself. "This is the wrong way to go about this," he said sternly. "You shouldn't get involved personally. This is a crazy idea. I don't want to know anything else about this if you're really going to go through with it." He was quite adamant.

O.J.'s sister who was standing there with us also chimed in, telling her brother it was not a good idea for him to be there personally. O.J. was loud and out in the open about it. He didn't care who heard what. "I've been looking for that stuff for years! They got my family photos, game-breaking balls, all my stuff!" Everyone could hear his rant.

O.J. introduced me to a white guy named Charlie who was around 50 years old and said he was the guy who was going to be posing as the buyer. That guy later turned out to be co-defendant Charles Ehrlich. My friend Lowell knew I was working with O.J. that week and wanted to meet the notorious football hero. I asked him to drop by the hotel while we hung out by the pool.

"Tom, I never pay for anything in my life," O.J. told me as we waited for Lowell. "I don't pay for this room, people line up to buy my meals. I haven't bought a drink in years. People think I'm so hated and despised. You saw what it was like out there at the pool. That's the way it always is. Everywhere I go, any bar or club, any limo or hotel, someone wants to pick up the tab. I never pay for anything." After what I'd just seen, I certainly believed it.

Lowell was running late, and O.J. decided he wanted to take a quick nap before we got on with our business. Lowell showed up a few minutes later and was anxious to meet O.J. Simpson. O.J. said it would be fine for us to come up to his room and take some pictures with my friend. He gave me his room number, and we headed up to O.J.'s room. As we got off the elevator and headed down the long hallway, we saw a woman exiting his room. When we drew closer, I realized it was O.J.'s longtime girlfriend Christine Prody. The lighting in the hall was dim, and it was absolutely freaky when we first saw her from down the hall. My friend and I looked at each other in disbelief because this woman looked just like a young Nicole Brown Simpson. It was pretty creepy.

We stopped and introduced ourselves when we got to the door. She started talking to us. "Oh yeah, Mike Gilbert, I know him. He offered me a million bucks to hide cameras and set O.J. up for a secret sex video. I told O.J. about it and he went off...." She rambled on about this incident for a while but was very nice to us.

O.J. Simpson and I in his hotel room at the Palms Hotel on September 13th 2007, hours before the incident in Las Vegas. Photograph by Lowell Katz.

After Christy left, Lowell and I went into the room. O.J. was flipping through the channels compulsively. Strangely enough, as soon as we sat down he launched into the same story about Mike Gilbert that Christy had just told us. Something about being sent money and moving the camera by mistake. A lot of people were mad at Gilbert because he didn't catch them having sex on the tape—all kinds of stuff like that. I wasn't following. I wanted to talk about what we were going to do that night.

O.J. said that Al Beardsley was a total douche who had literally stalked him in the past. He knew that Al was 6' 6" tall with a weight of about 300 pounds, but he wasn't afraid of him in the slightest and didn't care how big he was.

Since O.J. didn't want to have the meeting in his hotel room, we decided to rent a couple of rooms with connecting doors and meet at 6:00 p.m. O.J. would be in one room while I'd be in the other with Al and Charlie posing as the rich buyer of the stolen goods.

Then we dealt with the subject of my compensation: I
wanted him to autograph a bunch of his *If I Did It* books, but
he refused. "That's not my book now. The Goldmans got it
and changed things. I don't want anything to do with it," he
told me.

"You promised you'd take care of me. I've got
customers who need those books signed," I said.

"Anything but the book," O.J. said.

"Why not put the inscription THIS IS NOT MY
BOOK and then sign them?" I suggested.

"That's a good idea," O.J. said. "Okay, I'll do it."

We had a verbal agreement that I secretly captured
on a digital recording for him to sign 200 copies. The book
was supposed to be in bookstores that same day, but its
delivery to Las Vegas was delayed. By the time it hit stores,
we had other troubles. I never got my autographed copies.

Around 4:30 p.m. I got a call from O.J. saying,
"Change of plans, I don't want those guys coming over to my
hotel. Let's just do it at your place—no big deal."

Beardsley showed up at 5:30 p.m. and told me that
some guy named Bruce Fromong was coming instead of Mike
Gilbert. Bruce was another memorabilia dealer who was now
in possession of the stolen O.J. collection. He'd taken the
collection as collateral from Mike for an unpaid debt, and
Bruce wanted to sell it all.

Bruce showed up at 6:00 p.m., right on time.
Meanwhile I got a call from O.J. saying that he and his posse
were running late. I had no idea how many people were going
to show up.

Bruce and I went out to the parking lot. I examined
all the items in the truck and was surprised that you could
pile the whole collection in one trunk. Not everything on the
list that Al Beardsley provided was there, but certain
footballs and plaques that O.J. wanted were on hand.

O.J. called again to say he was running late, and I
warned him that the stash of stuff was kind of light, but he
made it clear that enough was there to make him want to go
ahead and try to get it back. Then his buddy Charles asked
to speak to one of the sellers, so I put him on the phone and
heard his loud raunchy voice shout, "Hey, I got the fucking
scratch, cash money. I hope you have all the shit."

Beardsley looked stunned. He was expecting to deal with a refined wealthy buyer and not Pauly Wallnuts from *The Sopranos*. I grabbed the phone before Charlie could spook Al and told everyone to go to my room.

These are some of the dress ties O.J. Simpson wore at his double murder trial in 1994. Al Beardsley tried to sell these items along with other stolen material the day of the incident in Las Vegas.

A bellboy brought the collection over to my room for us. I walked in first, turned on my small digital recorder, and placed it on top of the large TV cabinet. We arranged all the items spread out on the bed—O.J.'s stuff plus some other things they thought my "buyer" might be interested in, like Joe Montana lithographs and Pete Rose autographed baseballs. I even got a chance to take some pictures with my new iPhone of weird Al posing proudly with his collection of stolen O.J. crap.

I took this picture of Alfred Beardsley with one of O.J. Simpson's stolen game used footballs in my hotel room with my iPhone, just minutes before O.J. stunned him with his infamous surprise visit.

Al, Bruce, and I were sitting around my room and waiting for my big buyer to arrive. Al was really running his mouth, "This reminds me of a big drug deal I once did a few years back...."

"This isn't illegal," I reminded him.

"Everything about this is illegal," he said flatly.

Meanwhile it was now 7:00 p.m., and O.J. called again to tell me he was still running late. I told Al not to worry because our buyer was on the way. Bruce was pacing, talking on his cell phone, bugging me about where this guy was, and asking if I was sure he was coming. At one point one of them actually asked me, "O.J. or the police aren't coming, are they?" I laughed it off, but it actually did start to feel like a drug deal to me. Al was so nervous.

Bruce left the room to place a call. He came back in, gave me a hard look, and asked, "So Tom, what are you getting out of this?"

"I want a cut," I told him. "Let's say you want $20,000—better ask for 30 because I'm taking a third as commission for finding the buyer." The tension in the room eased a bit. They seemed more comfortable now that they thought I was interested in getting money out of this deal.

I finally got the call around 7:30 p.m. O.J. and his guys were in the lobby. "Give me your hotel room number, we'll be right there."

The Palace Station was a huge maze, and my room was hard to find. So I said, "Let me come out to the lobby and bring you to the room."

I told Al and Bruce that the buyer was here, and I'd bring him right up. When I got to the lobby, O.J. was there with five people including two white guys (Charlie and a guy I recognized from the pool party) and three black guys that I'd never seen before. Charlie came up to me and said, "So we're going to go in. I'll ask a bunch of questions...." He was acting like it was some big mob deal.

I knew the two guys waiting in my room had to be getting very nervous now. I decided I didn't want Charlie to even try to go into my room and pretend to be a buyer because it now seemed obvious that he knew nothing about the items or the business. He wouldn't know what to say, and there was a good chance he'd blow it.

I didn't want Al and Bruce to panic and run off, and I tried to calm Charlie down. "I'm 99 percent sure this is O.J.'s actual stuff. Let's just get O.J. to identify the stuff, and if they don't want to hand it over we'll call the cops. That's the deal."

Charlie thought that one over. "Stay here," he said and went back to the corner of the lobby where O.J. was surrounded by his posse. He wouldn't let me speak to O.J. directly. They conferred, and then they all came walking over together. They agreed to scrap the whole fake buyer idea and just confront the guys in my room about getting the stolen stuff back. They wanted me to lead, followed by the two white guys, and then the black guys with O.J. in the middle. They looked like a psyched up pro football team in complete game-face mode, leaving the locker room to do battle against the Raiders on Monday night football with O.J. still in the role of superstar.

We got to my room, and I opened the door with my key. A couple seconds behind me, the two white guys entered the room. There were some general greetings and "Hi, how are you" type of talk, and then all of a sudden the rest of the guys walked in. Bruce and Al's eyes almost popped out of their head when they saw O.J.

O.J. was pissed and let them know it right away. "You think you can steal my shit and get away with it?" O.J. was yelling, and you know what? Everything was actually going as planned—perfectly fine. Al and Bruce were completely cowed. They were happy to hand the stuff over to O.J. No problem! They were blaming the theft of the stuff on Mike Gilbert and were handing it over with apologies. That could've been the end of it, but then O.J. asked them to hand over their cell phones. Al didn't want to give his up, and at the same time Bruce objected to O.J.'s crew taking his Joe Montana lithograph by mistake along with O.J.'s crap. Then one of the black guys, later identified as Michael McClinton, pulled out a gun and that was it. There was no turning back at that point, because now a serious crime was needlessly committed.

I didn't know if the guy with the gun knew the whole story about how I was helping them get the stuff back. I was scared as hell. He waved the gun around, inches from my head. I never signed up for this!

O.J. was still screaming at Bruce, "You knew this was my personal stolen shit, and you never even tried to contact me? I told you 10 years ago I was looking all over for it!"

Al was backpedaling as fast as he could, "It was Mike! He stole it, not me!" But it didn't matter, things were out of control.

The guy with the gun was barking out orders while the others were packing all the shit in pillow cases and making nasty threats. Suddenly, one of the black guys told O.J. to leave, and they all left. It was all over in about five minutes, but the ramifications would last a long time.

Bruce turned to Al and said, "We were just robbed at gunpoint by O.J. Simpson! Call 911!"

Al grabbed the phone and dialed 911. Then both of them turned on me. Al said, "Man, you set me up, didn't you?" I didn't know if they were armed or not. I was alone with them, and O.J. was long gone. There was nowhere for me to go because we were in my hotel room.

The police weren't showing up fast enough for Al. He kept calling back every 30 seconds, howling into the phone, "I was robbed by O.J. Simpson! This is not a joke. Get the fuck over here!" A security man from the hotel showed up immediately, and the cops were in the room in less than 10 minutes. Then Al yelled at them in person, "You motherfuckers! He had a gun! What if we had been killed?"

"Wait a minute," one of the cops told him. "We got the call and it took us under nine minutes to respond. That's pretty good time. Besides," he took a look around, "it looks like everything's okay. No one's hurt. So calm down and we'll take a report."

Everyone started talking at once. Al launched into some whole explanation and actually admitted to the cops that he was dealing in stolen goods. I couldn't believe he confessed, "The stuff they took was originally stolen from O.J.'s trophy room about 10 years ago." I was surprised they didn't arrest him on the spot. More cops were showing up, and I knew this wasn't going to go away anytime soon. This was a big deal!

Thankfully the cops split us up. Al and Bruce were both pointing fingers and saying that I had set them up. We went out into the hallway, and I told the cops the whole story, exactly how it had happened. Meanwhile my cell phone was ringing, but obviously I couldn't answer it.

As soon as they were done with me, I checked my messages. Of course it had been O.J. trying to reach me. "Tom, man, I'm hearing stories that someone had a gun. That's not true. Don't say there were any guns because there was no gun!" That was the message. He was trying to convince me a gun wasn't involved, but that was ridiculous. I was standing right next to the guy with the gun. While I was listening to the message, he called again.

As soon as I picked up, he launched into the same speech without a break. "Tom, man, don't tell them there was any gun because there was no gun. Don't say there was a gun because there was no gun. It's cool as long as there was no gun." On and on he continued.

I interrupted, "O.J., I saw the guy waving that gun around."

"Did you tell the police that?"

"Yes, I told them that. It's the truth. I'm not gonna lie to the police!"

"You didn't tell them where I'm staying. Did you?" His voice was absolutely panicked. He seriously sounded ready to cry. "Are the police still there?"

"Yeah, they're still here, and more and more of them are showing up. There must be a dozen cops here now."

"Let me talk to the head guy in charge," he said suddenly.

That surprised me, but I found the cop who seemed to be in charge and held my cell phone out to him. "O.J. Simpson wants to talk to you," I said.

"Really?" the cop was surprised too, but he took the phone. They started talking, and next thing I knew I could hear O.J. laughing and joking. I couldn't believe how fast his mood had changed. The cop was laughing too! It was a very friendly chat for a few minutes.

"O.J. said there's no problem," the cop announced after he hung up. "He confirmed that he's at the Palms, and we can go by and interview him there." O.J. had turned on that famous charm once again. Suddenly the whole thing was no sweat, except for us. The investigation dragged on. I sat in the hall for a long time, and then finally they rented the room next door for me to stay in while Bruce and Al cooled it in the hallway for somewhere between seven and eight hours.

Midway or so into the investigation, one of the detectives read me my rights, and I was scared shitless he thought I had something to do with the gun play, but after I told him everything, the detective understood and let me go.

When they were finally done, they allowed me back in my original room to gather my belongings. I could not believe the state of my hotel room. It looked like a major crime scene. They collected my bed sheets; all the walls and furniture were covered with black fingerprint powder. Yellow crime scene tape was all over the door—you would have thought a murder had been committed. I went around collecting my things and headed slowly over to the large TV cabinet.

I noticed two large soda cups placed on top and immediately thought, *Oh shit! Did they find my digital recorder when the detectives placed those cups up there?* I placed my hand to the left of the first cup, no recorder. Then I placed my hand to the right of the second cup, still no recorder. I reached up to feel between the two cups and BINGO! There it was! The recorder was still running more than 10 hours after I'd placed it up there. They searched all night, nearly every square inch of my hotel room, except for the six inches between the Coke cups. If either one of those cups had been placed an inch more towards the center of the cabinet, they would have found the recorder. I was extremely lucky.

I grabbed my tiny digital recorder and stuck it in my pocket. Just then a detective came in and escorted me to a different room. It was a tough night, but things could have been worse. I was free and had the recordings to prove exactly what went down in one of the most famous "robbery" cases in U.S. history.

Chapter Twenty-Three

THE AFTERMATH
SEPTEMBER 2007

It was a long night of being questioned by detectives at the hotel, and when they were finished I looked out the window and noticed the sun was out. I checked my messages. O.J. had called over and over again. "Tom, did you listen to the news on TV? They're all saying that I broke into your room with a gun to rob everyone. You know that's not true Tom! You have to somehow set everyone straight. PLEASE!" O.J. was crying.

I turned on the TV and O.J. was not exaggerating. The early news reports were falsely accusing him of breaking into my room armed with a gun, but O.J. never broke into my room. I let him in and never saw him with a gun. I looked out my hotel window and across the parking lot a slew of media trucks and reporters were gathering to report this story. I wanted to set the facts straight before things got even more out of control. Although I was dead tired from zero sleep in almost two days, I went out to the makeshift media village and tried to fill them in on the facts.

"Look, my name is Tom Riccio. I had the room where the incident happened last night, and I just want to clear up a couple things. O.J. Simpson did NOT break into my room. He was invited to my room to retrieve items that were stolen from him by other guys, and O.J. did NOT have a gun." I explained.

One reporter asked, "Did anyone else have a gun?"

"Yes, but it wasn't O.J. That's it for now. I just wanted to clarify those things. I'm very tired. I need to get home and get some sleep. It's been a long night."

As soon as I got home to Los Angeles, the first call I made was to my lawyer Stanley Lieber. I started telling him this whole crazy Vegas story, but he broke in, "Let me guess, you taped this." Stanley has worked on a couple things where my tapes have come in handy by helping people "remember" exactly what they agreed to in a deal with me.

"Yeah I did," I said.

"I knew it! Okay, here's what you do. Very soon we will need to turn over this tape to the police, but don't tell anyone you have the tape just yet. Wait a couple of days and let everything ride. I'm sure the problems in your past are going to come out, then Bruce and Al will start spreading lies about you and turn the tables by saying that everything you say is a lie, that you're a felon, and so on. Let them lie for a few days and get it all out there. Then we'll produce the tape proving that your version of events is fair, accurate, and documented."

Wow, Stanley was right! The day after the incident, Bruce and Al had cut a deal with TMZ. Both of them claimed I had set everyone up and lied about everything. They said it was all a misunderstanding because Al and O.J. were great friends. O.J. himself went on the news doing interviews and telling everyone about his "self-organized sting operation" where he planned to retrieve his personal items.

I knew I had something important in that recording but was conflicted about how, if, or when to release it. I had only told my lawyer, but when my partner saw the news reports and called me, I thought he should also know about it.

Jeff shouted, "Holy shit! You have a tape of this whole thing? You know Tom, those clowns Bruce Fromong and Al Beardsley have completely thrown you under the bus. They're selling their stories to everyone in the media saying you lied about everything, and that it's all your fault because you set them up. How can you set someone up who knew they were dealing in stolen property? You need to trump them on this Tom. Let's make the best deal we can and get this tape out which accurately tells the whole story. They'll all know that the tape doesn't lie Tom. This is not a real good situation for you or our auction house. Let's do everything we can to turn this lemon of a situation into lemonade."

"Let me think about it Jeff."

O.J. called me and said, "Thanks for setting the record straight for me in the media Tom. I owe you, man." O.J. was always telling me that he owed me, but whatever it was he owed me I only seemed to be getting paid in headaches.

"O.J. you know I've had problems in my past and now it's all over the media. They're all calling me a slimy ex-con. This sucks for my family, and this can't be good for my business," I said.

"Tom, man, do you know who you're talking to? I'm O.J. Simpson! My life is one continuous soap opera. I've been though more shit in my life than anyone could ever dream of, and if there's one thing I've learned, it's that tomorrow you'll be yesterday's news and this whole thing will be forgotten."

I wasn't so sure. "O.J., I know you said there was no gun, but the problem was that I and everyone else saw a gun, and that alone makes this a big deal that I don't think can be swept under the rug."

"I never saw a gun, and I certainly never asked anyone to use one. I swear Tom! Would I lie to you man? Besides if anyone had a gun, they're not gonna tell on themselves so this is over and done with. I even got a hold of that nut Al Beardsley and gave him a little attention, so now he loves me again. We're friends. Al Beardsley is not going to say shit about me, and I know Bruce too. I'll take care of him, and this will all blow over. I've got everything under control. You'll see Tom. This will all be forgotten about soon. You'll be laughing about this and doing more business than ever within a week."

O.J. was wrong. One by one, most of his friends were turning themselves in to the police and admitting to their roles in the crime. Things weren't looking like this would go away anytime soon, and I wasn't sure if my recording would help or hurt him. I really didn't want the recording to be the thing responsible for putting O.J. in jail, because I knew it was just a small part of the big picture that could easily be distorted out of context. Without knowing the whole back-story, this recording could sound pretty bad for him. I was very conflicted on what to do with the recordings.

I tried to get my mind off the O.J. mess and dive into some business. I called Pete Kelly of Steiner Sports to get their inventory list of consignments for our upcoming auction. Peter stuttered, "Ah...Tom...Listen, we work hard here at Steiner Sports to bring memorabilia of sports heroes to the public, and O.J. Simpson just does not fit that profile. We can't afford to be associated with O.J., and in light of your current association with Simpson and this armed robbery in Las Vegas, we regret to inform you that we are cutting all business ties with you and your auction house."

I tried to explain that I wasn't charged with anything. It made no sense because anyone could sell their products. I just wanted to cut out the middle man and sell more Steiner items by dealing directly with them; however, they had already made their decision, and I lost this deal which cost my company millions in business and that was just the beginning.

I called Howard K. Stern about our upcoming Anna Nicole Smith Estate Auction, and he said, "Tom, I see all the stories about you on TV, and I'm really sorry about your problems. Believe me, I know exactly what you are going through. The media has really reamed me also, and now they're spreading all kinds of crappy rumors that Larry Birkhead and I are homosexual lovers! So you know, we just can't be associated with you and O.J. Simpson. I don't think it would work out now, for anyone."

I honestly couldn't understand why Steiner had pulled out of our deal because I could still buy their crap from other venders and resell them. It's almost like Wal-Mart coming to me and saying, "I'm sorry Tom, but we don't like O.J. so we won't let you shop here anymore." What the hell does my business supplier have to do with my association with O.J. Simpson? It was an unnecessary moronic decision by Steiner that hurt them as much as it hurt us, but Howard K. Stern's decision was one I couldn't argue with.

Howard and Larry Birkhead were severely criticized in the media and working with me with my now very public O.J. association would only add fuel to their already controversial public fire. I told Howard that I truly understood and wished both him and Larry the best of luck. That's the last I ever heard from them.

This was all getting worse by the hour. I was very upset that months of work had all gone down the drain due to all this O.J. bullshit, but I still was on the fence about releasing the recording. Then on Sunday, September 16, three days after the incident, the Las Vegas Police Department arrested O.J., and it was official: this was now a state case. My digital recording had nothing to do with O.J. getting arrested. It was all his friends coming forward with facts I knew nothing about that got him charged.

I sat there thinking the whole thing sucked. O.J. was now in jail, and I was losing tons of money everyday because my business reputation was destroyed when people heard I had a criminal record and served time. I made the decision to try and profit from this incident. Just then my partner called back, and I asked, "Hey Jeff, you still want to help me turn this lemon of a tape into some very profitable lemonade?"

Jeff came over within an hour and uploaded the recording to his laptop while I called TMZ and hinted that I had a recording of the now famous Las Vegas Caper. Harvey Levin called a special emergency meeting with us to negotiate a deal. My lawyer Stanley Lieber came with us to the meeting and made Levin sign a nondisclosure agreement promising not to talk about the digital recorder or its contents without an agreement in place. Once Harvey Levin signed our paperwork, we all sat down to listen to the recording, and I watched Harvey smile like a virgin in a whorehouse on free night. Problem was this wasn't free night! So I stated my price and watched his reaction change.

"TWO MILLION DOLLARS! Wow! Please tell me that's a joke," Harvey begged.

Harvey made us a counteroffer as ridiculously low as mine was high. We went back and forth. They made a few "last offers," and we threatened to leave and take the recording elsewhere. Every classic dealing tactic was used by both sides, but in this case, we knew that they wanted this recording as badly as we wanted to sell it. After they finally made a realistic counteroffer that we could live with, we took it. Done deal! The digital recording would be heard by millions of people within hours.

Harvey's popular website TMZ.com is the most popular gossip site in the world, and he was launching the newly syndicated *TMZ TV* show the week he bought our tape. The timing was right for both him and us to do well with this recording. I really like TMZ and Harvey Levin, and I'm certainly not offended by all his ridiculously low initial offers. If we hadn't gone through that two-hour ritual of dealing the way we did, I probably would have been very disappointed.

A lot of people have said, "That's tacky Tom. How could you sell this recording? You're going to ruin your credibility." What credibility? In most people's minds the only thing that has credibility is the recording. Even though I always tell the truth, no one would have believed me without this recording. I'm thankful I had it and did the deal with TMZ to release it.

Harvey and the TMZ staff were in a very celebratory mood after we struck a deal, and one of the guys on his staff told me a story of how TMZ had stolen a clip of Michael Richards, who played the Kramer guy from *Seinfeld*, at a comedy club going crazy and screaming "Nigger!" at everyone. He said they paid less than $10,000 for that clip which put them on the map and made them millionaires.

Everyone asked me, "Why won't you tell what TMZ paid you for your tape?" I wouldn't mind letting anyone know, but part of my deal was that I wasn't permitted to disclose the amount.

I asked Stanley, "Why do they care so much about the public finding out what they paid for a clip or photo?"

He explained, "If the public knew the amount of money they paid you, do you think they'd be able to continue stealing earth-shaking clips like the one they stole from that poor schmuck who had the Kramer Comedy Club tape?"

My lawyer said it was now time that we contact the Las Vegas Police Department to give them the original recording of the entire incident, but he also thought I might need immunity from any prosecution. Technically, I could be charged with temporarily withholding evidence or illegal taping. So, he arranged for immunity.

The police were thrilled that recordings existed—not just the 10 hours from the incident with O.J. in Las Vegas but tapes going all the way back to 2004 that had anything to do with Al Beardsley. After they checked out and confirmed my story about trying to contact the police and the FBI, they offered me immunity in exchange for my truthful testimony and all the evidence I turned over. I wanted to make it clear that I wasn't going to be classified as a witness for the prosecution or the defense. They agreed, and we had a done deal.

I knew Al Beardsley was insane but had no idea about his mile-long rap sheet full of dangerous stuff. Al had been charged with stalking a 63-year-old woman in California and as a result was deemed a high-risk parolee. This required him to check in with his parole officer by phone every day. I had thought for years he was a dangerous character, but I hadn't even realized how dangerous. Craig Rivera from *The Geraldo Show* told me that Al had been arrested for all kinds of weird stuff, even prostitution—soliciting it or selling sex himself. I couldn't figure that one out. I hope whoever bought his ass got change back from their nickel.

When it comes to some of my portrayals of Al Beardsley, many people will think that I'm being hard on the guy, but listen to anyone who knows him, the police, or portions of this following article from TheSmokingGun.com:

O.J.'S DELUSIONAL ACCUSER
The Smoking Gun, September 24, 2007

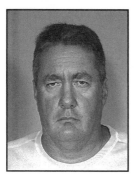

One of the memorabilia dealers who has accused O.J. Simpson of armed robbery was once so mentally unstable that he was jailed in a prison psychiatric ward. In fact, Alfred Beardsley's delusions included his belief that the ex-athlete and others were conspiring to "get" him.... Beardsley's criminal record...includes a 2004 felony stalking conviction,

prison time, and several restraining orders. But an incident in early-2000 may prove key to attacking the accuser's credibility in the Simpson case.... Beardsley was arrested on a pair of misdemeanor assault charges for trying to run another driver off the road. The fellow motorist was journalist Will Rogers, who had just written a story in California's Burbank Leader *newspaper about Beardsley's purported plan to run for city council. The story, which was skeptical about the wannabe candidate's political future, apparently set off the erratic Beardsley.... In an interview preceding the* Leader *story, Beardsley told Rogers that he was being harassed by Burbank's police, its city manager, and Mayor Stacey Murphy, whom, Beardsley claimed, was stalking him and "spreading false rumors that they are having an intimate personal relationship...." Beardsley also explained that he "hears voices" urging him to become mayor immediately, "to win control of the Burbank Police Department...." Then Beardsley focused on Rogers, who he insisted was "in on it," according to the journalist's affidavit.... "He said he believes I am now joined with—or that I am perhaps leading—efforts by Burbank's Mayor and O.J. Simpson to 'get him.' Beardsley then asked Rogers, "How did they get to you?" and "Who put you up to this?" ...During his* Burbank Leader *interview with Rogers, Beardsley claimed that he was Simpson's personal assistant and managed the ex-athlete's memorabilia....*

*   *   *

It sucks that when Al is able to hold it together for a few minutes in an interview, most people believe his "delusions." He went on a television show after the incident and said, "I'm very upset that Tom Riccio didn't get arrested." I must have gotten 100 calls and e-mails from media outlets about that remark, all asking the same thing, "Al Beardsley is very upset that you didn't get arrested! Are you worried about an impending arrest?" or "Al Beardsley said your tape is doctored."

I tried to realize that not everyone knows how nuts Beardsley is, but I was still very pissed that they were quoting Beardsley as if he were the president of the United States. Over and over, media people everywhere validated their stories with "Al Beardsley said...." Shame on them!

Once something is out on TV, radio, magazines, or newspapers, it practically becomes the gospel truth. I'd never realized how true that was until this incident happened. Anyone can say anything ridiculous to the media and next thing you know it's on 30 shows, and then blatant lies will suddenly become the gospel truth in everyone's eyes.

I taped most of my interactions concerning Al Beardsley because he was and is a scary loon. I recorded this incident in Vegas not because of O.J., but because Al was involved. If he went nuts on me or anyone around me, I wanted a record of it. If he denied the goods were originally stolen, I had plenty of evidence that he knew they were.

Beardsley finally got arrested on the parole violation, so for now, he's not making any more media appearances, but the damage was certainly done.

Chapter Twenty-Four

NATIONWIDE MEDIA CIRCUS
SEPTEMBER-OCTOBER 2007

I'd had business dealings with O.J. Simpson in the past, and they had gone very smoothly. He was always good to me and very friendly. But would I ever cover up for him? No. On the flip side, am I trying to help put him behind bars? No. The fact is I was only involved with helping O.J. retrieve his stuff without a conflict. I don't know what he planned on the side, but there were never any crimes discussed with me. That's never been disputed by anyone, and everyone who knows me knows that I'm not into violence and would never allow a gun in my room.

It's considered robbery in every single state in this country when someone takes something by force using a gun. The whole crew got charged with robbery because of their association and proximity to that one gun. Some reports claim there may have been a second gunman in the room, but I only witnessed one.

One of those guys involved was a hotel bartender they'd picked up a few minutes earlier! He was just some guy getting off work. They probably said to him, "Hey, come party with us. We're going to make one stop and pick up some stuff." Everybody would agree that he had no idea what was going on, but the poor slob got charged with robbery nonetheless.

Almost immediately after the whole O.J. incident hit the airwaves, it was reported that one of the guys in O.J.'s mob was his longtime golf buddy Walter Alexander. News reports claim that he was the second gunman in the room the night of the crimes. Alexander has a long violent rap sheet and was charged with robbery and kidnapping years ago, but he got let off the hook because the victims were too afraid to testify. When Alexander read that I got immunity, he was the first of O.J.'s gang to approach the police about making a deal. I got my immunity because the police knew I was not involved in any plot to commit armed robbery; however, Alexander admitted his involvement.

Alexander still tried to make his case to the media that I was the sole reason for all his problems. Everywhere I turned, he was on TV dressed up, holding his prop of a Bible in his hand, and telling the reporters that I'd set him up and then turned on O.J. Once again, I couldn't believe how fast the media spread his obvious bullshit all over the news like he was Reverend Martin Luther King spreading the word of God.

I often wonder why great news people don't expose frauds like Walter Alexander on the spot. Isn't it obvious to the average person that Alexander brought a gun with him out of his own free will? Alexander himself admitted that I never even met him until he came to my hotel to commit his crimes. So how could I have set him up? Why didn't any reporter challenge him when he sat there acting like a victim and blaming me for turning on O.J.? This guy was just trying to turn the tables to get the heat off of him, and the media played right into it. I thank God that the police at least know the truth. By now, it's known by everyone that I had nothing to do with the armed robbery. Alexander admitted that he was a key figure in the crime and armed with a gun. It's very ironic that Walter Alexander is pointing the finger at me for turning on the gang, but I can't take the credit for that because I was never part of O.J.'s gang. I was merely a business acquaintance. In fact, it's easy to see that if there's a close friend of O.J.'s that turned out to be his rat, it's none other than Walter Alexander.

Most of the media haven't been real nice when reporting about me. I know the world wants villains they can easily hate. I fit that jacket, but what really bothers me is how phony a lot of the media is. They treat me nice when they're courting me to come on their show, but then they bash me when a negative story comes out. Why not be honest and bash me while they are interviewing me? I would appreciate the chance to respond to their allegations live and not just hear them after I'm off the show.

One of the most persistent reporters in the business is Geraldo Rivera. He and his staff can be a pain in the ass at times, but I like them. When the Anna Nicole Smith Diaries story broke, I was bombarded with press requests. Geraldo's brother Craig works closely with him and invited me on the show. I was happy to accept the invitation. They always kept their promise by allowing me to mention my sponsors. I went on a few more times for follow-ups, and all my appearances worked out well.

We stayed in touch, and Geraldo called every now and then to see what was going on in my business. Then just after the Vegas O.J. incident, he called me up and said, "You've got to come on my show today Tom!"

"Geraldo," I told him. "I just got back from Vegas and I haven't slept in days, literally. I'm wiped out. It's my daughter's birthday, and I'm home at her party. I can't do it."

Geraldo kept insisting. "We'll send a limo. We'll give you some time to prepare."

"I am not leaving this house tonight, no way." I should have known better than to argue; Geraldo doesn't take no for an answer.

"Fine, we'll send someone there with a microphone. It'll just take a minute of your time."

"Can't do it today, Geraldo," I explained for what seemed like the tenth time."

"Okay listen," Geraldo persisted, "I just heard about how you were an ex-con. I never knew that. Look, I know you. You're a good guy. I'll talk good about you on the show. People will know how you've always been straight up with me, and that everyone needs to believe your story."

Geraldo hit a nerve with that remark. This was the one thing I really cared about. He was offering me a chance to rehabilitate my reputation and would speak well of me. I was taking a real beating in the press. Even my mother back in New Jersey was calling me to cry about it.

"I want to take you up on that, but not today Geraldo. Can we do this in a couple days? I'll have a big story for you then." I was thinking about the release of my recording of the incident, but I couldn't even tell him at that time. "I've been talking to my lawyer, and he said I should break this out in a day or two. Trust me, this is huge! You're gonna want to have me on your show after this comes out. Let's talk about it on Monday."

"Bullshit Tom! There's no bigger story in the world than this. O.J. was involved in a robbery in YOUR room. I need you on the show today. Just please, do me this favor. We'll come out with a little remote and do a fast interview."

"Okay, Geraldo," I gave in. "You can send someone over real quick, but like I said, it's my daughter's birthday. Please make this low profile."

"Yeah, yeah, fine." Click.

Geraldo hung up, and minutes later, a caravan of cars and trucks lined up on our street with generators, satellite dishes, and technicians all over my lawn saying, "We're going to do a live remote!" They did exactly what I didn't want them to do—interrupt my daughter's birthday party.

The 30 or so kids at my house eating cake for Angela's party couldn't believe it. They kept asking my daughter, "What did your dad do?"

"Oh shit!" I said to Geraldo's brother Craig. "I thought this would be one guy with a camera and a microphone. Geraldo's turning this into an international event!"

He kept his word and assured viewers that I was a reputable businessman. Then Geraldo got me on the show and grilled me like I was the guy with the gun, but the minute it was over, he acted like he was my best friend. "That was great buddy, get back to your daughter's birthday party, and give her my best wishes. I won't bother you anymore."

I kept telling him. "Wait a few days Geraldo, I'll have a much bigger and better story for you."

"Tom, nothing will ever be bigger than this in your life," he said. "This is as hot as it gets, and we wanted to be first. Nothing you can say or do will outshine this."

A couple of days later, when the recordings were released and made worldwide headline news, I got a call. "I see all over that you've release a recording of the whole actual incident. I guess that's the big news you wanted me to wait for," Geraldo said in a deadpan voice.

"No Geraldo, I have pictures of me, Elvis, and Marilyn Monroe in a spaceship! Can you have me on to speak about our ride together to planet Zotar?"

Dead silence. Geraldo was afraid to doubt me again. "Really?" he asked.

Later on, I see my old nemeses Al Beardsley on *Larry King Live* spewing the same old crap he sold to every other show. "Riccio set everyone up in his seedy cracker box hotel room. I know he's a con artist who once again conned everyone. He doctored those tapes so that everyone would get into trouble while he's making millions." Then weird Al Beardsley tossed in a great new sound bite. "Riccio works for Howard K. Stern and Tom Cruise," he proclaimed on the worldwide broadcast show.

Once again why didn't anyone say, "Why the hell are you even saying that crazy crap on my show?" But no, they accepted it as gospel.

Larry King announced that he was running out of time but was having Beardsley on tomorrow to finish his story. I immediately thought, "I want to go on!" and called CNN. They agreed to have me on the show with Beardsley. I told the *Larry King* producers that Al would never go on the show with me, because he knew I would expose him for the nut he is.

The producer told me, "We can't ambush Beardsley. We have to let him know you are coming on. This is not *The Geraldo Rivera Show*!" They were right about that.

When I showed up for the show, I was informed that Beardsley was given a photo of me and told I would be joining him on the show. He took one look at my picture and ran out of the studio. I did the show without Beardsley, and Larry King was great. I remember sitting up at night as a kid listening to his show on the radio after the Yankee games. It was cool to meet him.

I had a recording from inside my hotel room right after the O.J. incident where Bruce Fromong could be heard screaming that he had hidden money for O.J. in offshore accounts. In addition to not knowing Bruce and having nothing against him, a lot of people in my business had told me he's not a bad guy—so I'd stopped my partner from making that recording public.

At first I was very happy I hadn't released it, because a couple days after the incident Bruce had a heart attack. I felt bad for him and his family, but two days later, Bruce got out of his hospital bed to go on every show to tell lies and bash me. My partner called and said, "Are you still feeling sorry for this asshole, or can I finally release the tapes of him that will bite him in his ass?"

"Release the hounds!" I ordered Jeff.

The recordings of Bruce Fromong proclaiming that he'd set up illegal offshore accounts for O.J. Simpson were released to TMZ.com and played everywhere. Larry King had Bruce on the same show as Harvey Levin of TMZ, but Larry King did not put him on the same segment with Harvey Levin to speak about the incriminating recording. Harvey was openly shocked that they wouldn't confront Bruce about it, and once again Larry King's producers missed the boat by not taking advantage of a good opportunity. Where the hell is Geraldo Rivera when you really need him?

Howard Stern is probably my favorite celebrity. I was happy to go on his show and got to mention that Clips4sale.com had audio clips of the O.J. Vegas incident on their website. I made a nice payday for that appearance.

Other radio shows and magazines called including the *National Enquirer*. I had a cool conversation with an editor there. He told me they used to own the *Weekly World News* which was like a hilarious over-the-top parody of the *National Enquire* that would feature stories like "Hillary Clinton has Affair with Space Alien" and a black & white front page photo showing the strange embrace of our former First Lady with a space creature.

Most people never understood that the stories in the *Weekly World News* were not intended for people to believe. They were just to entertain us. I was sad when the editor informed me that the publication had closed down, and the last issue had gone out that week. I was even more upset when he said that he would have featured a cover photo of me and O.J. chasing Big Foot for stealing our stuff. It's too bad because I would have bought 1,000 copies, and maybe they'd still be in business.

Chapter Twenty-Five

LAS VEGAS/REFLECTIONS OCTOBER 2007 - JANUARY 2008

My friend Lowell wanted to move to Las Vegas. Houses were cheaper there, and he loved all the action. He finally got his wish and relocated. I see him whenever I'm in Vegas and still hear from him all the time. One day the phone rang: "Hey, I'm a limo driver in Vegas now, and I invented a new idea that's gonna make me rich: The Love Limo! I put it on this new site called Craig's List. 'Have a passionate, hot, intimate encounter with your girlfriend while cruising the Strip!' and it's working Tom. I had a guy the other night who paid me extra because his girlfriend gave him head while they cruised. I'm glad I thought of this. The Love Limo is gonna drive me to Easy Street!"

Soon enough someone called him up about his Love Limo advertisement and tried to book him, but Lowell didn't have a limo that night. He tried to explain, but the guy was insistent on doing it that night. Since he was promising Lowell crazy money, Lowell called his brother-in-law Eddie and said, "I've got a customer who has an emergency need for my Love Limo service, but I don't have the Limo today. So bring over your SUV as soon as possible."

The brother-in-law showed up in a crappy old SUV, but the guy didn't complain. He got in and said, "Hey, where the bitches at?"

"Um, I don't know. You're supposed to bring your own," Lowell said. "The Limo of Love is so customers can be driven around and do what they want in privacy. We came here, but we never promised to supply any girls."

"So, where are all the working girls?"

"Well," Eddie pointed out, "We're in Vegas. They're everywhere!"

"Okay, let me make a call, then take me to the Golden Nugget. I'm going to pick one up."

They took him to his hotel, and he came out with some woman. As soon as they were settled in the back seat and back on the Strip, the guy asked, "Okay, where can we get high?"

Eddie said, "I have no idea."

"Well, we gotta score some hash. Where can I get some?"

"Listen, you've got this totally wrong. We don't know where the drugs are at. I don't think you understand this whole Limo of Love idea."

"Look, just take me back to that same hotel, and I'll find some myself." They drove him back, and as soon as the SUV pulled into the parking lot, it was surrounded by a half dozen Las Vegas vice cops. Lowell and Eddie were arrested and charged with all kinds of things: pimping, pandering, promoting illegal sex practices, and transportation of prostitutes. You name it, and they got charged with it. The police love to pile on the charges in Vegas.

Lowell called me later and was in tears telling me this whole story. I said, "That sucks Lowell. It sounds like the charges are really excessive, but you had to know something was gonna happen with this. It was a great idea, but if it were legal, people would already be doing it."

"Ah, it's all right. I'm getting a lawyer. I'll deal with it." Lowell hired an attorney named Robert Lucherini and paid him a large retainer, but Lowell soon called to complain about him. According to Lowell, Lucherini missed several court dates, had breath that stank from alcohol, appeared to be so hung over that he could barely function, and scared the shit out of Lowell by telling him he was facing years in prison.

Meanwhile the brother-in-law, who couldn't afford to hire an attorney, wound up with a great public defender. "Don't worry, this is crap. We'll get all this dropped," the public defender assured Eddie. He made a deal for Eddie to get a misdemeanor and pay a $50 ticket.

This sent Lowell into a complete tailspin. "Look, can't you just get me the same deal my brother-in-law got?" he asked. Eventually Lowell got the same deal, but he had to ask the judge himself. Lowell was steamed and said paying Lucherini's fee was the worst money he ever spent.

A few months later in mid-November, I was in court for the O.J. Simpson preliminary hearing. Some very sloppy looking lawyer got up to cross-examine me. He was the lawyer for defendant Clarence "C.J." Stewart and started asking me all kinds of irrelevant questions, "Did you ever record people in other states? Did the FBI also grant you immunity?" This asshole did nothing for his client, and it was obvious he was just trying to stir up attention with the FBI to see if they would play into his game of harassing me. I was very upset.

That night I went to play poker with Lowell, and he said, "Hey Tom, I saw you on TV and guess what? Do you remember that jerk-off incompetent asshole of a lawyer I had in the Love Limo Case, Robert Lucherini?"

This is me in November 2007 with Judge Joe Bonaventure Jr. at O.J. Simpson's preliminary hearing in Las Vegas. I was a key witness at the hearing where O.J. was bound over for trial on 12 felony charges including kidnapping and armed robbery.

Photo: Getty Images News Collection/Getty Images

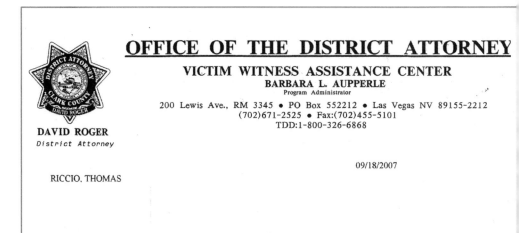

OFFICE OF THE DISTRICT ATTORNEY

VICTIM WITNESS ASSISTANCE CENTER
BARBARA L. AUPPERLE
Program Administrator

200 Lewis Ave., RM 3345 ● PO Box 552212 ● Las Vegas NV 89155-2212
(702)671-2525 ● Fax:(702)455-5101
TDD:1-800-326-6868

DAVID ROGER
District Attorney

09/18/2007

RICCIO, THOMAS

PLAINTIFF: STATE OF NEVADA
VS.
DEFENDANT: SIMPSON, ORENTHAL JAMES
J.C. FILE NO: 07F19284A
CHARGES: MJR VIOLATRS UT

A criminal complaint was recently filed in the Clark County Justice Court against the above named defendant. You have been included on the witness list for this case and you may receive a subpoena from the District Attorney's office. The subpoena will indicate a date for a preliminary hearing, which will determine if there is enough evidence to try the defendant on the charges.

If you are subpoenaed someone from our office will contact you to make all the necessary travel and hotel arrangements.

In order to better serve you, please keep us informed of any changes in your address, phone number, or place of employment. Please indicate any changes on the pre-addressed card, which is included so we may update our records. Our office can provide various services to meet your needs as a victim/witness, such as language interpreters and accommodation of physical needs.

A victim/witness advocate is assigned to this case to assist you as the case proceeds through the court system. If you have any questions, have sustained any injuries, property damage or loss, due to this crime, please contact us at 702-671-2525. We will assist you or refer you to the appropriate agency.

DAVID ROGER
DISTRICT ATTORNEY

BY: BARBARA L. AUPPERLE
     PROGRAM ADMINISTRATOR

"Yes Lowell, you only complained about him every day for two months." I said.

"Well that ugly moron who was giving you a hard time in court today was him. Robert Fucking Lucherini!"

The next day in court, Lucherini asked me for the identity of my limo driver friend who was on the digital voice recorder while I was in O.J.'s hotel room the day of the incident. I couldn't believe it! This guy had no idea he was asking for the name of a former client who hated him. I now understood why Lowell despised Lucherini so much. I also knew that Lowell didn't want to be identified at that point and bringing Lowell out as another character in this case was not something I wanted to deal with. It's not that I'm embarrassed by Lowell. I just didn't want to see Lowell's mug shot next to mine and every other schmuck in this case. So, I asked to keep his name anonymous.

"I want to know who was your friend who was with you that day in O.J.'s room," Lucherini pressed further. He was just a bystander who only wanted O.J.'s autograph and had nothing to do with any of this shit, but Lucherini would not let up.

I was tempted to say, "It was your old client Lowell Katz! Remember him? He had nothing good to say about you!" Eventually the judge agreed that Lowell's identity didn't matter, and his name could stay out of the whole affair, but after the hearing, the prosecutors demanded that I identify Lowell. He went in and told his story. Lowell then allowed me to tell his story of his experience with Lucherini.

I made it clear when I took my "deal" in which I was granted immunity that I wasn't going to be a witness for either the prosecution or the defense. I was just going to tell the truth, and I refused to shade my testimony one way or the other to help either side.

To the dismay of the defense, I knew there was a gun in the room. I saw it! To the dismay of the prosecution, I had absolutely no knowledge that O.J. had any prior knowledge a gun was there, or even if he actually saw the gun when it came out because he had been several feet in front of the guy with the gun, facing Fromong and Beardsley while screaming at them.

The problem is someone pulled out a gun and

technically committed robbery. The big question is: Did O.J. know about it? Did he have any idea this would happen and did he plan it? I don't know the answer to that because I was never in on any of the group's planning sessions and wouldn't even want to speculate on it. It seems like all the people who were in on these plans will tell everyone exactly what happened at the trial. The plan we originally went with was fine with me until the guns came out, and that's what I said.

I was surprised because the defense especially treated me respectfully and didn't even bring up my past. I was expecting a lot worse.

After I was completely finished testifying, O.J. stood up. I looked directly into his eyes, and he actually smiled and gave me a little wave. I didn't know what to expect; I hadn't spoken with him personally since the day before he was arrested in Vegas, back when he was reassuring me it would all blow over soon. No hard feelings it seemed, and there shouldn't be. I did everything I said I would. I just never wanted to be involved in what turned out being an armed robbery.

Given what a nut Al Beardsley is, I thought he came off pretty well on the stand. Only about 25 percent of his craziness showed through. He contradicted himself endlessly; his story changed from minute to minute, but he held himself together.

No one knows how this will all play out, but for some reason EVERYONE wants to know what I think should happen and up 'till now I've refrained because I didn't think that my opinion should count. I'm not the judge, and I'm not in the jury, but people seem to think that my views on this case would not be complete without conveying my thoughts as to how this should all turn out.

I think that just about everyone except the bartender who was asked to carry up the boxes is guilty of something here. I don't believe O.J. wanted anyone to get hurt. I know he only wanted to get his personal shit back, and he believed that there was no other recourse than to do it the way he did. So with that in mind, I would hand down two separate judgments for O.J.

1. If O.J. didn't know guns would be involved in this incident, I would only find him guilty of some small

misdemeanor for the over-the-top intimidation he displayed on Fromong and Beardsley and sentence O.J. to probation.

2. If it is proven that O.J. did lead a conspiracy to have guns involved in this incident, I would find him guilty of some of the charges but not all of them and definitely not kidnapping—nobody was kidnapped. O.J. was only in the room about five minutes and left without taking any hostages after he got his crap back. I know he never intended to hurt anyone. With the finding of guilt for the gun conspiracy, O.J. should probably do some sort of prison time, but certainly nowhere near the life sentence he is now facing.

Ever since this incident in Las Vegas happened, media blitzes on the story have come and gone in waves. It was like a tidal wave when it first happened, and the number one question was, "Why didn't you just go to the police if you had a problem with someone regarding stolen goods?"

I answered that question in my first interview with Geraldo when I told him that I went to the police and FBI weeks before the incident, but they refused to get involved. I went on dozens of other shows and even showed the business cards the FBI agents gave me but still nobody cared.

Things died down for a few weeks, and then about six weeks after I first told everyone about my meeting with the FBI, the *Associated Press* released a report that the FBI confirmed I'd met with them three weeks before the incident to ask for their help in catching the people who were selling O.J. Simpson's stolen goods. A whole new wave of media blitz occurred. Every show reported this information as if it was brand new, including shows that I'd been on weeks before to personally provide that same information. I'm still waiting for the day when the media starts giving my statements some kind of credibility. Hell, I'd be happy if they gave me at least as much credibility as they always seem to give psycho Al Beardsley, but I won't hold my breath waiting for that to happen.

What finally happened to all of O.J.'s shit that he wanted back so badly? All the stuff wound up in police custody and will presumably go to the Goldmans. The Brown family also have a 25 percent claim on whatever is recovered by the Goldmans, as well as O.J.'s kids. "At least my kids will get 25 percent," O.J. told me way back at the beginning when we were first planning this. If they weren't gonna hand it over voluntarily, we would have just called the police anyway. How ironic?

It was also ironic how much this arrest helped the confiscated book *If I Did It* immediately become a bestseller. It was forecast for doom, but the arrest and the insane media frenzy that followed was what drove its success and here's how I feel about that: Good for them! I'm all for anyone making money. I'm always happy to hear of anyone's success, and if this incident somehow helped anyone, including the Goldmans, then maybe we actually accomplished something.

I personally wouldn't have taken a million dollars for my reputation, credibility, and business to have taken the hit that I did, but it happened. I would never be a phony and lie about my motives. I am out to make as much money as I can off this incident. Whatever people think about that, I don't care.

I am in a business where people entrust me with hundreds of thousands of dollars in valuable merchandise to sell and having myself brought out everywhere as a felon was not a good thing. I was finally feeling comfortable because it was 13 years since I'd last been in trouble. I figured the past was the past, and no one would ever bring it up again. Well, not so.

They say bad things happen in threes. When I lost both the Anna Nicole Estate Auction and the big Steiner Sports consignment deal, I couldn't help but wonder what was next. Jeff and I were working with a company called Superior Coins out of Beverly Hills, California. Superior consigned a few odd and exciting pieces that we thought would cross over to our high-end memorabilia customers. Things like complete penny sets, $500 bills, $1,000 bills, ounces of gold, and silver bricks. Our relationship was very successful for both of us, but then superior got bought by a company called Dallas Gold and Silver.

The CEO of Dallas Gold and Silver was a real friendly Texan who was very interested in diversifying his coin auction with a memorabilia auction. We immediately talked about a merger where he would buy our company, and we would work with him to establish a memorabilia auction by bringing our consigners over to his high-end customers.

Everything was going well, and it looked like it was all going off without a hitch until this O.J. incident.

I was surprised that the CEO did not seem affected with the whole O.J. case, but by December, when the deal was about ready to go through he said, "Tom, you know we really like you and Jeff a lot, and I also want you to know that I'm a big supporter of bringing you on, but I have to let you know that we are a publicly traded company that has to let our shareholders know when we're bringing on an ex-felon to be an executive in charge of a new division. But in the end we decided that the shareholders just don't know you as well as we do, and it wouldn't be a good idea to ask them to approve of you with your record. We all feel it just wouldn't fly, so why even bother? I hope you understand."

"So is that it?" I wanted to know. "No chance of us doing anything with you guys after almost a year of working on this merger?"

The CEO went on to explain that there would be only one way: If they could take only Jeff to start their memorabilia division, they would certainly do it. However, they wouldn't ask him unless they had my approval.

I thought about it for a while and knew that all the deals we were losing were because of me and my past. We weren't gonna do well anyway. Why block Jeff from an opportunity to work with a great company like Dallas Gold and Silver?

I knew Jeff is a natural when it comes to running a memorabilia auction house, and it's what he loves doing. He and his wife Sunny are having a new baby in a few months, and this is an opportunity he shouldn't pass up. After three years together at our auction house, we both decided that I would step down and close Universal Rarities so that Jeff could go run the memorabilia auctions at Dallas Gold and Silver. I wished them all the best of luck.

*   *   *

The year 2007 was strange for me; I ended 2006 by visiting my dad who had Alzheimer's. My mom did everything in the world to take care of him for six years with

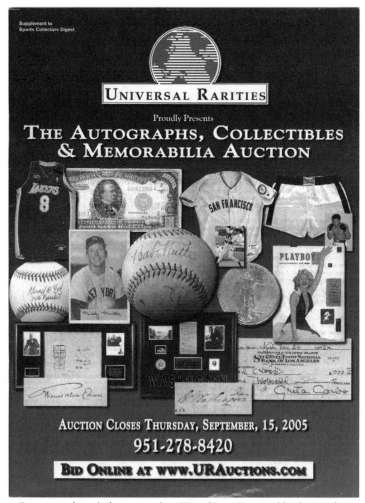

This was our very first catalog from my auction house "Universal Rarities." It was a sad day when I recently learned that our merger did not go through, and so Universal Rarities' three-year run has come to an end.

this horrible disease, but by October of 2006, she had to place him in a nursing home due to her own failing health.

It was very strange to see my dad at Christmas. He was about the smartest guy I ever knew, but now he didn't even know my name. After I went home, I got a call from my brother Paul on New Year's Eve, and as I answered the phone, I felt a very dark cloud come over me and asked, "Did Dad die?"

Paul said "No, we all just went to see him, and I just called to wish you and your family a Happy New Year." He hung up the phone, and five minutes later, he called back to tell me that my dad was dead. We spent the beginning of the New Year going back to New Jersey for my dad's wake and funeral.

One of the weirdest events of my life was seeing my dad in a casket with 100 friends and family walking around like it was almost normal. Every once in a while, a person who I hadn't seen in years would come up and greet me and maybe even reminisce about a story from my youth which would make me smile for a second, but then I'd see my dad's body out of the corner of my eye and get depressed. The loss of my 86-year-old father was pretty devastating, but I knew that his first 80 years were full of great accomplishments, and he had the love of my mom for over 50 years to help him raise 9 successful kids.

*   *   *

By the end of 2007, just about everyone knew that I was involved in both the Anna Nicole Smith scandal and the O.J. mess. I was receiving lots of strange phone calls from all kinds of people. My phone rang from a private number and a man's voice asked, "Is this Tom Riccio?"

"Yeah, who's this?"

"Never mind who this is. What would you say about a tape of Britney Spears committing suicide? The actual tape? Can we be partners? What do you think? Can we make a million dollars? More than the O.J. tape?"

"Oh my God, Britney Spears committed suicide?" This had to be a prank. I couldn't believe it; I knew she was having some well-publicized problems, but how could I have missed this?

"Oh, it hasn't happened yet, but it's going to, and I'm in a position to get it on tape. How much can we make?"

"Wait a minute guy! Why aren't you calling the police or her family or trying to prevent it rather than have a video camera ready for something like that?"

The guy cursed me and hung up. Thank God it seems to have been just a crank call, but you never know with the shit that comes my way—Anna Nicole, O.J., and then

Britney. But I'm not interested in handling something like that anymore. My auction house is closed. I am out of the celebrity bullshit trade.

As 2008 started, a new wave of O.J. crap hit the fan. O.J.'s bail bondsman Miguel Pereira reported to the judge that O.J. had tried to contact a co-defendant. The judge revoked O.J.'s bail, and Pereira was granted permission to go to Florida to pick up O.J. and bring him back to jail for a new bail hearing.

Pereira went to Florida and got on a plane with the talkative O.J. while taping their every word with a digital recorder. Gee, I wonder where he got that idea from.

I just found out on January 28, 2008, from a Las Vegas criminal investigator that Pereira's recording contains an admission by O.J. that he did in fact order the thugs who came into my room to bring guns. If that's the case, I don't see how he could walk from all this, but stranger things have happened.

*   *   *

People are telling me how other people are using recorders to entrap celebrities and sell their recordings to gossip sites. Dog the Bounty Hunter's son recorded some derogatory remarks that Dog made to him in a phone conversation, and Dog's son ended up selling the tape to the *Enquirer* for $15,000. A lot of people are asking me how I feel about this new wave of celebrity recordings, and you might be surprised by my answer: I think it all sucks! First of all, I would never turn my dad in no matter what he did, and second of all, I think it's disgusting to try to befriend a celebrity just to get some dirt on them and sell it to the gossip columns. I've taped situations for many years to protect myself in a few deals where I felt there was a strong possibility that someone may burn me.

Now that I no longer have my auction house I will continue to deal memorabilia on the Internet and with my many business friends I have here in Southern California. Even though I have lost most of my new business contacts, I consider myself lucky to have dozens of old contacts that still consider me a friend.

Many of my business friends congregate every Wednesday and Saturday at the local Frank & Sons Collectible Show, owned by Frank and Janet since the 1980s. I still go there regularly to buy, sell, and have my memorabilia framed.

One day I'm walking around the Frank & Sons Show, and everyone is wearing a "Tom Riccio Fan Club" button which features my mug shot from the last time I was arrested back in the 1990s. It was kind of alarming at first, but I thought it was funny and knew that most of the people there liked me.

I know that I truly am a different person than I was even just a few short years ago. All my life, nothing was ever enough. I always wanted the next thing, and then I thought I'd be satisfied. I couldn't wait 'till I got to high school, and once I got there, I thought life would be great, but it wasn't enough. Then I thought that once I got a car life would be great, but it wasn't enough. My whole life was always like a great parade, but I never enjoyed what was marching in front of me. I always was stretching my neck to see what was coming down the street.

I couldn't wait to graduate and get my own place. Life would really be great for me then, but I still wasn't happy. Then I needed to get $50,000; then no, it had to be a $100,000; then no, the only way I could be happy and set is if I had a million dollars, but that wouldn't do it for me either.

I knew what the answer would be. I needed a nice beautiful wife and my own family, but even that wasn't enough. I needed to buy a big house and put 11 big screen TVs in every room; but no, I wasn't finished. I had to get my own auction house and constantly look for every crazy way-out deal that was gonna make me another fast million. It never seemed to be enough.

Just recently my oldest daughter turned 18, and I've realized that my life is flying by. I never took the time to stop and enjoy it. At 45, for the past few months since this incident, I have slowed everything down and reflected on my entire life. A few weeks ago my book publisher said that we only have a few weeks to get this book in under deadline, and I realized I've really enjoyed spending late nights here on my computer writing and reflecting on every aspect of my life.

Sometimes I sit and watch the Biography Channel where I see the life stories of all kinds of people. I'm always interested to see just how many successful people have come from the humblest of beginnings. I know that not everyone in this world is blessed with opportunities. Some people in different countries have a hard time just figuring out where their next meal will come from, but most of us here in this country have the opportunity to do whatever we want.

I wake up now, late every morning, roll out of bed, listen to my messages, and eat a brunch. I go to the phone and spend a couple of hours making a few deals to try and raise just a few bucks each afternoon. Then I eat a great meal with my family, watch some TV, and spend a little time with Irene before I call it a night. That's a typical day for me now, and I enjoy it. Most days I don't even leave my house, and I'm fine with that. I finally found my secret to life, and it's not really having what I want, but it's learning to want what I have.

Like Steve Martin's character Nathan in one of my favorite movies *The Jerk*, I have been from rags to riches and back to rags again more times than I can remember. Irene and I have had our ups and downs, and I know that all the ups have been because of her and all the downs have been because of me. Even though we have been divorced for about 10 years and she is technically my ex-wife, we have been together most of our adult lives. I am very thankful for that.

As I'm sitting here finishing up this book, Lowell has called me from Vegas and is blabbing in my ear about his next big get-rich-quick scheme, but I have a deadline and will save all that for my next book!